Cyber Shield

PALMETTO
PUBLISHING
Charleston, SC
www.PalmettoPublishing.com

Copyright © 2024 by Dr. Torrez Grace, CISSP, Dr. Jamaine Mungo, CISSP, and Dr. Lewis Pate, CISSP

All rights reserved
No portion of this book may be reproduced, stored in a retrieval system, or transmitted in any form by any means–electronic, mechanical, photocopy, recording, or other–except for brief quotations in printed reviews, without prior permission of the author.

Paperback ISBN: 979-8-8229-3208-1
eBook ISBN: 979-8-8229-3209-8

Cyber Shield

A Comprehensive Guide to Enterprise Cybersecurity

By: Dr. Torrez Grace, CISSP
Dr. Jamaine Mungo, CISSP
Dr. Lewis Pate, CISSP

About the Authors

Dr. Torrez L. Grace is a seasoned cybersecurity thought leader, educator, and IT management professional with more than twenty years of leadership experience in information security, information assurance, and security operations. He has worked in program/project management and software and telecommunications network/system design, development, engineering, testing, fielding, operation, and maintenance. Dr. Torrez L. Grace is an effective communicator and organized planner and has motivated teams to complete jobs on time and on budget, from initiation to launch. He is a U.S. Air Force veteran with an extensive record of high-profile duties in military cyber security operations.

Dr. Jamaine Mungo is an accomplished cybersecurity security professional, an alumnus of Virginia State University, and an educator with over twenty years of experience in cybersecurity. He has implemented next-generation cyber strategic initiatives, delivering advanced technology concepts along with researching cybersecurity risks and automated remediation solutions. A highly valued expert in his field, Dr. Jamaine Mungo has presented to industry security leaders, participated in cyber research, and examined real-world cases regarding cybersecurity risks. He holds several industry security certifications. He is a professor at Cornell University teaching various cybersecurity courses. He has a strong passion for education, innovation, and technology.

Dr. Lewis Pate has over twenty years of international experience spanning eleven countries in the areas of cybersecurity, IT application delivery, IT infrastructure design, IT security management, project management, and cyberspace operations. Lewis has held several leading positions with multinational companies in both the public and private sectors. He held roles as chief technology officer, cybersecurity operations center director, and information assurance portfolio manager for the US departments of the Air Force and Space Force. His excellent performance record includes leading numerous large-scale project teams to seamlessly deploy business solutions while demonstrating his ability to integrate disparate technologies, processes, and people to produce strategic alignment of IT solutions with business goals and objectives.

Please visit their website for additional information.

Website: https://www.anatomyofcyberattacks.com/cybershield

About the Authors: https://www.anatomyofcyberattacks.com/authors

Email Contacts:

Dr. Torrez L. Grace, CISSP: torrezg@yahoo.com

Dr. Jamaine Mungo, CISSP: jamainemungo@icloud.com

Dr. Lewis Pate, CISSP: Cyberalist@gmail.com

Executive Summary

Developing a comprehensive cybersecurity defense strategic plan for a large corporation is a complex task that requires a deep understanding of the organization's business goals, assets, and risks. To achieve this goal, it is crucial to conduct a comprehensive risk assessment that identifies vulnerabilities, threats, and potential consequences for the business. This should cover both internal and external factors that may affect the organization.

In addition to risk assessment, it is important to develop a security policy and governance framework that ensures that all employees, contractors, and vendors are aware of the organization's cybersecurity objectives and adhere to them. This governance framework should also include a process for monitoring compliance and enforcing consequences for noncompliance.

Access control measures should be implemented to restrict access to sensitive data and systems. This should include authentication, authorization, and encryption technologies to ensure that only authorized individuals can access the organization's critical assets.

To address potential cyberattacks, it is essential to develop an incident response plan that includes procedures for detecting, analyzing, and responding to security incidents. This should also include communication with stakeholders such as customers, partners, and regulators.

Conducting regular security awareness training for all employees, contractors, and vendors is another key element in protecting an organization's assets. This training should educate them on how to identify and respond to potential cybersecurity threats, including simulated phishing attacks and other types of social engineering attacks.

Implementing security measures to protect the organization's network infrastructure, including firewalls, intrusion detection and prevention systems, and network segmentation, is crucial to maintaining network security. Endpoint security measures to protect the organization's devices, including anti malware, encryption, and patch management, are equally important.

With the increasing adoption of cloud infrastructure, it is also essential to implement security measures to protect the organization's cloud infrastructure, including identity and access management, encryption, and vulnerability management.

Third-party risk management is another important aspect of cybersecurity defense for a large corporation.

It is essential to implement a third-party risk management program to ensure that vendors and partners meet the organization's cybersecurity standards.

Continuous monitoring and threat intelligence programs should also be implemented to proactively identify and respond to potential cybersecurity threats. Finally, developing a disaster recovery and business continuity plan ensures that critical business functions can continue in the event of a cyberattack or other disruptive event.

To ensure compliance with relevant laws, regulations, and standards, such as GDPR, HIPAA, PCI DSS, and the NIST Cybersecurity Framework, it is essential to establish compliance measures as part of the cybersecurity defense strategy.

In summary, this prioritized cybersecurity defense strategic plan covers the key areas of cybersecurity defense for a large corporation. However, it is important to note that cybersecurity is an ongoing process that requires continuous monitoring and improvement to ensure that the organization's assets are protected. By implementing this plan, a large corporation can establish a solid foundation to protect itself from cyberthreats.

Contents

About the Authors   i

Executive Summary   v

Introduction   1

Chapter 1: Introduction to Cybersecurity for Enterprises   3

Chapter 2: Risk Assessment and Threat Modeling   10

Chapter 3: Developing a Cybersecurity Strategy   22

Chapter 4: Incident Response Management   26

Chapter 5: Continuous Monitoring and Threat Intelligence   30

Chapter 6: Secure Cloud Computing   34

Chapter 7: Risk Assessment A Comprehensive Exploration of Its Significance and Process   53

Chapter 8: Incident Response Planning   75

Chapter 9: Identity and Access Management   85

Chapter 10: Third-Party Vendor Risk Management   97

Chapter 11: Security Awareness Training   105

Chapter 12: Employee Education and Awareness   126

Chapter 13: Regulatory Compliance and Governance   134

Chapter 14: Continuous Improvement and Assessment   145

Conclusion   157

Introduction

In today's digital age, cybersecurity is critical to the success of any enterprise. Cyberattacks can cause significant financial, reputational, and legal damage, making it essential for businesses to develop and implement robust cybersecurity strategies. This book serves as a guide to developing an enterprise cybersecurity plan that will help businesses protect their assets, data, and reputation from cyberthreats.

Furthermore, this book covers various aspects of cybersecurity, including risk assessment, threat modeling, security policies and procedures, protection of networks and infrastructure, cloud computing, mobile device security, endpoint security, identity and access management, incident response planning, security awareness training, vendor and third-party risk management, regulatory compliance and governance, security operations and monitoring, and continuous improvement and assessment.

Dr. Torrez L. Grace, Dr. Jamaine Mungo, Dr. Lewis Pate

As a discerning business leader navigating the dynamic landscape of the digital era, you find yourself at the crossroads of innovation and vulnerability. In the relentless pursuit of success, the intricate dance between business expansion and cybersecurity resilience has never been more critical. This book invites you, the visionary business owner, the strategic executive, the astute manager, and the vigilant IT professional, to embark on a transformative journey towards fortifying your organization's cybersecurity posture. In an age where data breaches and cyber threats loom ominously, the insights within these pages will empower you to not only comprehend the intricacies of modern cyber challenges but also to wield the knowledge needed to safeguard your enterprise. This is your handbook for navigating the intricate maze of cyber risks and emerging triumphant in the realm of digital defense. Welcome to a narrative that unfolds the strategic playbook for a secure and resilient future.

Chapter 1:
Introduction to Cybersecurity for Enterprises

In this chapter, we provide an overview of cybersecurity and its importance for enterprises. We define key cybersecurity terms and concepts, including "threat," "vulnerability," "risk," and "attack." We also discuss the current state of cybersecurity threats and the potential consequences of cyberattacks for businesses. Finally, we provide an introduction to the cybersecurity framework and its application to enterprises.

In the context of cybersecurity, a threat is any potential event or action that could exploit vulnerabilities in a system or network, leading to harm, damage, or unauthorized access. Threats include various forms of malicious activities such as hacking, viruses, phishing, and insider attacks. In today's technology-driven world, large organizations face an array of information cybersecurity threats that require comprehensive strategies and programs to manage information security risk. Cybersecurity breaches and data theft incidents often result in financial losses and reputational damage for an organization. Therefore, developing and implementing an effective information security strategy and program is vital for large organizations to protect their critical assets and ensure business continuity.

A vulnerability is a weakness or flaw in a system, network, or application that can be exploited by a threat actor to gain unauthorized access, disrupt services, steal data, or cause other forms of damage. Vulnerabilities can arise from software bugs, misconfigurations, poor security practices, or outdated technology. Vulnerability management is the proactive approach of identifying, assessing, prioritizing, and addressing vulnerabilities in computer systems, networks, applications, and other IT assets within an organization. It involves a systematic process to manage security weaknesses that could be exploited by attackers to compromise the confidentiality, integrity, or availability of information systems. This entails actively scanning IT systems and networks to identify potential vulnerabilities. There are several ways this can be accomplished: using automated vulnerability scanning tools, manual testing, or a combination of the two.

This testing often reveals software flaws, system misconfigurations, weak passwords, insecure network protocols, or other weaknesses that could be exploited. Once vulnerabilities are identified, they need to be assessed to determine their potential consequences and likelihood of exploitation. This includes evaluating the severity of each vulnerability, understanding its potential consequences, and assigning it a risk rating or priority level. Vulnerabilities are prioritized based on their severity, exploitability, and potential effects on the organization. This helps organizations focus their resources and efforts on addressing the most critical vulnerabilities that pose the highest risk.

After prioritizing vulnerabilities, organizations develop a plan to address them. This plan may include deploying software patches, updating configurations, applying security controls, implementing secure coding practices, and any other necessary measures to mitigate the identified vulnerabilities. Vulnerabilities are then addressed through various means such as applying patches, making configuration changes, updating software versions, and implementing other security measures. This step aims to reduce or eliminate the risk associated with the vulnerabilities. Moreover, vulnerability management is an ongoing process, as new vulnerabilities are continually discovered and new systems are deployed.

Continuous monitoring and periodic vulnerability scans help ensure that any new vulnerabilities are promptly identified and addressed. Throughout the vulnerability management process, it is important to maintain records of vulnerabilities, assessments, remediation actions taken, and those actions' outcomes. Documentation helps in tracking progress, reporting to stakeholders, and demonstrating compliance with regulatory requirements. By implementing an effective vulnerability management program, organizations can significantly reduce the risk of security breaches, improve their overall security posture, and protect their critical assets from exploitation by malicious actors.

Another significant concern for large-scale organizations is cybersecurity risk. This includes technical, operational, and strategic risks and the ways they can affect an organization's overall security posture. In order to address these risks, organizations must understand the importance of assessing risk, as it forms the foundation of effective cybersecurity strategies. Risk assessment is the process of identifying, analyzing, and evaluating potential risks and vulnerabilities within an organization's digital infrastructure. Conducting regular risk assessments provides the ability to proactively identify and address potential vulnerabilities, allocate resources effectively, comply with industry regulations, and maintain the trust of customers and stakeholders.

A cyberattack is a malicious and deliberate action carried out by individuals, groups, or organizations, aiming to compromise or disrupt computer systems, networks, or digital devices. The primary objectives are gaining unauthorized access to data, inflicting harm, stealing valuable information, or undermining the security, confidentiality, or accessibility of digital resources.

Cyberattacks can cause significant financial losses, reputational damage, and legal liability. In addition, organizations have a responsibility to protect the sensitive information of their customers and clients. A data breach can have severe consequences for both the organization and the individuals affected. Cybersecurity should be a top priority for all organizations, regardless of their size or industry. By implementing robust security measures and providing regular cybersecurity training to employees, organizations can significantly reduce the risk of a data breach.

In today's digital age, it is not a question of whether an organization will face a cybersecurity attack but rather a question of when. Consequently, understanding, mitigating, and accepting cybersecurity risk is crucial for large-scale organizations to ensure their survival and success. Our aim is to provide an expert-level overview of the key principles and best practices for developing and implementing cybersecurity strategies and programs for large enterprises.

Cybersecurity is the practice of protecting computer systems, networks, and digital assets from unauthorized access, use, disclosure, disruption, modification, or destruction. Cyberthreats can come from various sources, including hackers, criminals, nation-states, insiders, and even accidental actions by employees. Enterprises need to take a holistic approach to cybersecurity to protect their assets, reputation, and customers' trust.

Cybersecurity is essential in today's digital world. Because of the ever-growing threat and sophistication of attacks, cybersecurity is becoming more and more important, so much so that experts in the field of cybersecurity view it as one of the most critical components of modern security.

Although traditional security methods still play a role, they are inadequate on their own. As more businesses store confidential information online, they become increasingly vulnerable to cyberthreats. Developing a comprehensive cybersecurity defense strategic plan for a large corporation is a complex task that requires a deep understanding of the organization's business goals, assets, and risks. To achieve this goal, it is crucial to conduct a comprehensive risk assessment that identifies vulnerabilities, threats, and potential consequences for the business. This should cover both internal and external factors that may affect the organization. In addition to conducting risk assessment, it is important to develop a security policy and governance framework that ensures that all employees, contractors, and vendors are aware of the organization's cybersecurity objectives and adhere to them. This governance framework should also include a process for monitoring compliance and enforcing consequences for noncompliance.

In recent years, cyberattacks have become more sophisticated and frequent, causing significant financial, legal, and reputational damage to businesses. Cybersecurity incidents can result in data breaches, loss of intellectual property, system downtime, financial fraud, and legal liabilities. These consequences can have long-lasting effects on the business, including loss of customers, damage to the brand, and regulatory fines.

To address these challenges, enterprises need to develop and implement robust cybersecurity strategies that align with their business goals and risk appetite. The cybersecurity framework provides a structured approach to managing cybersecurity risks and enables enterprises to establish a common language for communicating about cybersecurity risk management. The first part of a cybersecurity plan is assessing risks and developing a threat model.

Chapter 2:
Risk Assessment and Threat Modeling

In the ever-evolving landscape of today's interconnected digital world, as cyberthreats continue to grow in sophistication and prevalence, adopting a proactive approach to safeguard critical assets has become imperative for enterprises. This chapter delves into the intricate process of conducting a comprehensive risk assessment and developing a robust threat model. These practices hold paramount importance in systematically identifying potential risks, vulnerabilities, and threats that organizations are susceptible to. Through a meticulous risk assessment, businesses can effectively recognize cybersecurity risks and vulnerabilities, and a well-structured threat model enables them to anticipate potential threats along with their associated tactics, techniques, and procedures.

Asset Identification and Evaluation in a Cybersecurity Context

Imagine a prominent financial institution that depends substantially on its digital framework to orchestrate crucial transactions and safeguard highly sensitive customer information. In this illustration, the institution's valuable assets encompass an array of components, most notably customer databases housing a trove of personal data, the complex web of transactional systems facilitating monetary exchanges, and the intricate landscape of online banking applications that empower seamless user interactions.

Within the realm of cybersecurity, the meticulous process of risk assessment assumes a pivotal role. This multifaceted procedure encompasses a thorough exploration of potential vulnerabilities that could compromise the institution's digital fortifications. These vulnerabilities span various dimensions, including the lurking perils of outdated software, the vulnerabilities unveiled by insufficiently fortified access controls, and the latent frailties concealed within the intricate tapestry of the network architecture.

In our real-world context, envision a scenario in which outdated software within the institution's infrastructure unwittingly creates a chink in its digital armor. This weakness could be exploited by malicious actors to infiltrate the network, potentially leading to data breaches or unauthorized access. Similarly, inadequate access controls might inadvertently grant unauthorized personnel access to confidential financial data, exposing the institution and its customers to significant risks.

To make matters worse, the panorama of vulnerabilities extends beyond the realms of software and access controls. A comprehensive evaluation must also grapple with the looming specter of natural disasters. For instance, consider the effects of a catastrophic event such as a severe earthquake or a devastating flood that could render critical infrastructure inoperable. Without contingency plans in place, the institution could find itself grappling with not only financial repercussions but also the erosion of public trust.

Adding another layer to this tapestry of risks is the ever-present concern of accidental data leaks. A single misconfiguration or lapse in protocols could precipitate the exposure of confidential customer information. The fallout from such an incident could reverberate far beyond financial ramifications, potentially plunging the institution into a quagmire of legal troubles and resulting in a tarnished reputation.

Thus, the meticulous identification and evaluation of assets and their associated vulnerabilities form the bedrock of a resilient cybersecurity strategy. The financial institution's digital landscape is akin to a fortress, and the risk assessment process functions as the vigilant guardian, ensuring that potential weak points are diligently scrutinized and fortified. In this intricate dance of proactive protection, the institution can mitigate risks, strengthen its digital bulwarks, and engender a climate of trust that resonates with its customers and stakeholders alike.

Risk Evaluation and Impact Analysis in the Cybersecurity Landscape

Let's delve into the realm of risk evaluation and impact analysis. In this complex digital landscape, conducting a meticulous risk assessment involves understanding the intricate balance between potential threats and their consequences.

Picture an e-commerce juggernaut that heavily relies on its online platform to drive substantial revenue. In the case of this e-commerce giant, a risk evaluation encompasses a comprehensive examination of multiple factors. Specifically, let's consider the menacing specter of a distributed denial of service (DDoS) attack. In this scheme, a threat actor orchestrates a massive surge of traffic aimed at overwhelming the company's website, rendering it incapacitated and unavailable to its customers.

To contextualize further, let's draw parallels to real-world incidents. Imagine a situation in which an e-commerce giant is hit by a large DDoS attack during a peak shopping season, perhaps Black Friday. Legions of compromised devices, acting as a botnet, direct an avalanche of traffic toward the website. This triggers a cascade of adverse effects: the platform's responsiveness plummets, transaction processing grinds to a halt, and the website becomes effectively inaccessible. This could lead to a substantial loss of potential revenue as customers, frustrated by the experience, abandon their shopping carts or take their business elsewhere.

Now, the impact assessment comes into play. The repercussions extend far beyond just financial losses. The brand's reputation takes a severe hit, as news of the incident spreads across social media and tech news outlets. Customers, wary of potential security vulnerabilities, might think twice before entrusting their personal information to the compromised platform. The company might also find itself facing legal actions from customers whose data might have been compromised during the attack.

To put this into perspective, let's draw from history. The 2016 Dyn DDoS attack is a prime example. In this infamous incident, a colossal botnet executed a crippling assault on the Domain Name System infrastructure, affecting numerous popular websites and services, including Twitter (now known as X), Netflix, and Reddit. This attack not only resulted in financial losses but also had far-reaching implications for the companies' reputations and the broader perception of online security.

For business leaders, addressing cyber risks necessitates a strategic balance between likelihood and impact. Risks that boast both a high likelihood and substantial impact demand immediate attention and proactive mitigation strategies. In our e-commerce scenario, a successful DDoS attack exemplifies this convergence. Robust defensive measures, such as traffic filtering, load balancing, and partnerships with DDoS mitigation providers, become paramount to safeguard the business's digital operations.

In essence, the interplay among risk, likelihood, and impact underscores the multidimensional nature of modern cybersecurity. It's a dynamic landscape where astute professionals employ their expertise to predict, prevent, and mitigate threats, ensuring the resilience and continuity of businesses in the face of an ever-evolving digital threat landscape.

Threat-Modeling Process

Imagine you're steering a ship through uncharted waters, and the journey is your company's pursuit of success in the technology landscape. In this context, the threat-modeling process becomes your compass, helping you navigate through the intricate currents of cybersecurity risks.

Let's explore a tangible example to truly grasp its importance. Consider a cutting-edge technology start-up that's on the cusp of launching innovative internet of things (IoT) devices, i.e., smart thermostats, appliances, TVs, and other Wi-Fi-enabled technology. These devices have the potential to revolutionize how people interact with their environments, making them a prime target for various cyberthreats.

The threat-modeling process in this scenario is akin to setting up an advanced security system for your start-up's headquarters. It involves not only setting up locks and cameras but also understanding who might want to break in and why.

In the cyber realm, we identify potential threat actors, which are the digital counterparts of burglars, spies, and even saboteurs. These threat actors could include your competitors, who may want to steal your groundbreaking ideas and research to get a competitive edge. Cybercriminals might also be eyeing your technology, hoping to exploit vulnerabilities for financial gain. Furthermore, nation-state actors could be interested in your IoT device because of its potential military or strategic implications.

Understanding these actors' motives is crucial. Just as you'd assess whether a burglar wants to steal valuables or sabotage operations, we analyze whether threat actors are aiming for industrial espionage, financial exploitation, or even disruptive actions.

Once we have this insight, it's like having an early warning system in place. We can anticipate and prepare for the tactics, techniques, and procedures these threat actors might employ. Think of it as predicting whether a burglar would pick a lock, smash a window, or hack a security system to gain access to your headquarters. Similarly, we aim to predict whether cybercriminals will use malware, phishing attacks, or other methods to compromise your IoT device's security.

By proactively understanding these threats, we can design robust defenses. Just as a secure building layout and advanced security measures deter potential intruders, a well-prepared cybersecurity strategy can thwart attackers' efforts, protecting your technology, your data, and your business reputation.

In conclusion, the threat-modeling process isn't just a concept—it's your strategic advantage in the world of cybersecurity. It ensures that your innovative IoT device doesn't just set sail; it sets sail securely, weathering the storm of potential threats and emerging stronger, safer, and more successful in the ever-evolving digital landscape.

Attacker Identification and Analysis

Attacker identification and analysis stands as a sentinel guarding sensitive digital assets. Imagine a health-care institution as a fortress housing valuable patient records. Just as physical castles have faced threats from a diverse array of adversaries throughout history, a digital fortress encounters a wide spectrum of potential attackers in the cyber realm.

Consider cybercriminals, modern-day marauders who eye patient data as a lucrative commodity to peddle on the black markets of the internet. These assailants are driven by financial gain, aiming to exploit the personal and medical information of patients. By understanding their motives, we not only anticipate their tactics but also equip ourselves to counter their advances.

Yet a digital fortress isn't besieged only by profit-driven intruders. Enter hacktivists, digital vigilantes with political agendas. Their motivations stem from a desire to disrupt or manipulate an enterprise's operations, aiming to gain visibility for their causes or ideologies. Their attacks can manifest as attempts to compromise systems, steal data, or even publicly expose vulnerabilities. To protect against this, we must decipher their underlying intentions and craft proactive strategies that mitigate risks.

By meticulously analyzing potential attackers—their motivations, tools, and capabilities—we unveil a chessboard of potential scenarios. This foresight empowers us to gauge the likelihood of breaches and unauthorized access, making the invisible threats more visible. Just as a skilled military general studies the terrain to anticipate enemy movements, we study the digital landscape to predict and thwart potential breaches.

In this pursuit, our analysis serves as a compass, guiding us toward fortifying our defenses. As we uncover potential vulnerabilities that attackers might exploit, we gain the upper hand. Each insight becomes a building block, shaping the decisions that define our security measures and access controls. Imagine these insights as the blueprints to construct an impenetrable fortress, safeguarding customer data and ultimately their trust.

In conclusion, our role as cybersecurity stewards involves understanding the diverse cast of characters who might assail a digital bastion. By discerning their motivations and capabilities, we arm ourselves against a myriad of threats. This knowledge is the bedrock upon which our decisions are founded—decisions that determine the allocation of resources, the design of safeguards, and the calibration of our response strategies. Just as a vigilant watchman surveys the horizon for signs of danger, we peer into the digital horizon to protect, defend, and uphold the sanctity of our institution's digital realm.

Likelihood and Impact Evaluation

This section provides a detailed and business-oriented explanation of the importance of cybersecurity, specifically focusing on the concepts of likelihood and impact evaluation.

In today's interconnected digital landscape, the security of an organization's operations is paramount. Let's delve into a practical scenario that underscores the significance of assessing both the likelihood and impact of potential cyber incidents. Imagine a multinational corporation that relies heavily on cloud services to streamline its operations. This reliance on the cloud introduces both immense opportunities and critical vulnerabilities.

When we as cybersecurity professionals evaluate the likelihood of a cloud service outage, we don't merely speculate. Instead, we base our assessment on a comprehensive analysis of factors that contribute to service reliability. We scrutinize the track record of the company's service provider, examining their historical performance to understand their ability to maintain consistent service levels. We also delve into redundancy measures they have in place—backup systems and failsafe mechanisms that ensure continuity even in the face of technical glitches.

Furthermore, we take lessons from past incidents into account. By analyzing similar incidents that have affected the cloud service landscape, we gain insights into potential vulnerabilities and weaknesses that might expose the company to similar risks. This practice ensures that our evaluation is grounded in real-world experience, enhancing the accuracy of our predictions.

The second facet of our assessment is evaluating the potential impact of an outage. This isn't just about technological disruptions; it's about understanding how such disruptions would ripple through the company's global operations. We weigh the potential loss of productivity, the financial implications of halted operations, and perhaps most crucially, the potential damage to the firm's hard-earned reputation. In today's interconnected world, a single security incident can quickly tarnish the trust a company has built with its customers and partners.

Now, consider an outage with a high likelihood and significant impact. Such a scenario demands more than just hope—it necessitates action. This is where a robust business continuity plan comes into play. An enterprise must be prepared to seamlessly transition to alternative systems or providers, ensuring that operations continue uninterrupted. Additionally, contingency measures need to be well defined, enabling staff to effectively manage the crisis and minimize its consequences.

In the grand scheme of a cybersecurity strategy, this meticulous assessment process is foundational. Real-world examples underscore the tangible effects of this approach. By understanding and categorizing potential risks and vulnerabilities, organizations and their staff are empowered to proactively address them. Likewise, the construction of a threat model, a detailed analysis of potential threat actors and their tactics, techniques, and procedures, equips enterprises with the foresight needed to anticipate and counteract emerging threats.

As you assimilate these insights, you will be better positioned to create strategic cybersecurity plans that don't just react to incidents but also actively prevent them. Your approach will evolve from merely safeguarding data to safeguarding your business continuity, your reputation, and the trust your stakeholders place in your company. By dedicating yourself to these practices, you not only mitigate risks but also enhance the overall security posture of your organization.

In the dynamic realm of cybersecurity, we recommend that rigorous risk assessment and the construction of a robust threat model serve as your guiding lights. They empower you to make informed decisions, enabling you to protect your operations and reputation with steadfast confidence. Embrace these practices as the cornerstones of your cybersecurity strategy, anchoring your organization in a landscape of constant change and evolving threats.

Chapter 3:
Developing a Cybersecurity Strategy

In the fast-paced landscape of modern business, the importance of robust cybersecurity strategies cannot be overstated. This chapter delves into the intricate process of crafting a security framework that serves as a proactive shield against the multifaceted landscape of cyberthreats.

Foundation in Risk Assessment and Threat Modeling

At the core of every effective cybersecurity framework lies a meticulous risk assessment and comprehensive threat modeling. This intricate process forms the bedrock upon which all subsequent strategies are built. The blueprint as designed is akin to a digital fortress, aimed at safeguarding critical assets and sensitive data from potential cyber adversaries.

Engineering Policies and Procedures: A Crucial First Step

The development process is initiated by establishing precise security policies and procedures. This segment involves delineating access controls, devising stringent password protocols, formulating data-backup methodologies, and orchestrating incident response strategies. These protocols, driven by insights from risk assessment and threat models, must be subjected to periodic revisions to maintain their efficacy in the face of evolving threats.

Technological Integration: Bolstering Defenses

No modern-day stronghold is complete without advanced technological components. Similarly, security frameworks must integrate cutting-edge measures. Think of these technological assets as sentinels deployed to the ramparts. Firewalls are like the castle's moat and drawbridge, thwarting unauthorized incursions. Intrusion detection and prevention systems serve as vigilant guards, continually patrolling for any signs of a breach. Antivirus software is the digital equivalent of a medical ward, protecting the system from infections. Encryption technologies serve as an impervious cloak, rendering sensitive data indecipherable to malicious actors.

Human Element: Empowering the Front Line

Even the most impregnable of walls can be compromised if the gatekeepers are unaware. Employees form the front line of defense, and their awareness is paramount. Regular training programs are essential to arming them with knowledge. They learn to discern phishing attempts, devise strong passwords, and promptly report breaches, thus reducing potential vulnerabilities.

Proactive Vigilance: Regular Security Assessments

Incorporating proactive evaluations into the framework mirrors medieval siege drills. Regular assessments and testing simulate real-world attack scenarios, helping to identify potential weaknesses. Penetration testing replicates a siege attempt, pinpointing potential entry points. Vulnerability scanning serves as the equivalent of scouting for cracks in the castle's walls. By subjecting the framework to such proactive evaluations, organizations can shore up vulnerabilities before they are exploited.

Sustaining a Culture of Advancement: The Pursuit of Excellence

A cybersecurity framework is not static; it must evolve to remain effective. Continuous enhancement is imperative. Regularly analyze the results of security assessments and testing, adjusting strategies accordingly. Respond to shifts in the threat landscape and embrace emerging technologies and best practices. A forward-looking approach ensures that the framework remains adaptive and resilient.

A Comprehensive Blueprint for Modern Businesses

To summarize, the vitality of a meticulously designed cybersecurity framework cannot be overstressed. Rooted in risk assessments and threat modeling, this blueprint combines security policies, advanced technologies, well-informed personnel, proactive assessments, and a culture of perpetual advancement. In the next chapter, we delve into the art of incident response and management. In an era defined by digital transformation, the safeguarding of business interests hinges on an unyielding commitment to cybersecurity excellence.

Chapter 4:
Incident Response Management

As we venture deeper into the realm of cybersecurity strategy, it becomes increasingly apparent that incident response planning and management are the linchpins of an enterprise's defense. In this chapter, we'll delve into the intricacies of incident response, unveiling its critical role in safeguarding your business operations and reputation.

The Strategic Foundation: Incident Response Planning

At its core, incident response planning serves as our battle strategy in the ever-evolving landscape of cyberthreats. Think of it as the playbook that guides your actions when confronted with an attack. Picture an elaborate chess match in which every move is calculated, every contingency considered. To draw a parallel, an incident response plan is your chessboard, allowing you to strategically maneuver in response to any threat.

The Ensemble of Experts: Building the Incident Response Team

To effectively execute a plan, you must assemble an incident response team (IRT) similar to a symphony orchestra, in which every instrument has a distinct role yet harmonizes with the others. Your IRT should include members from various departments: IT, legal, human resources, and public relations. Their various areas of expertise mirror the diverse instruments in an orchestra, creating a harmonious response to any incident. Regular training and practice sessions serve as rehearsals, ensuring that when the incidents occur, the IRT is able to properly contain, mitigate, and remediate cybersecurity incidents.

The Choreography of Crisis: Navigating an Incident

Imagine a cyber incident as a storm at sea. Your incident response plan transforms chaos into choreography. Once the IRT is activated, each member plays a key role. IT isolates affected systems, legal navigates regulatory waters, HR prepares for potential effects on personnel, and PR scripts transparent communication. This orchestrated response not only limits damage but also exemplifies your commitment to security and customer trust.

Decrypting the Incident: Analysis and Recovery

Beyond containment, the plan mandates thorough analysis. Incidence response analysts dissect the incident, unveiling its origins and extent. This forensic process aims to unmask the adversary and fortify the business's defenses. It's akin to deciphering the artistry of a painting's brushstrokes, understanding the attacker's technique to bolster your own. The preservation of digital evidence is paramount; it's your trail of breadcrumbs, leading you back to the source.

The Post Incident Debrief: Enhancing Resilience

The aftermath of an incident is a critical moment of reflection. The IRT conducts a post-incident analysis, similar to reviewing game footage after a match. This process illuminates your company's strengths and exposes your vulnerabilities. The insights gleaned serve as the foundation for refining your incident response plan, making your business ever more formidable against future threats.

Cultivating a Sentinel Culture

Cybersecurity is more than just technology; it's a mindset. Imagine the crew of a ship all trained to mend sails in a storm. Similarly, every employee should have a basic understanding of cybersecurity best practices. This cultural shift involves providing regular awareness programs, empowering your employees to be a line of defense, acting as human firewalls and watchful sentinels guarding the digital kingdom.

Technological Guardians and Ongoing Vigilance

In tandem with an effective incident response plan, cutting-edge security technologies stand guard. These digital watchdogs are in sync with the plan, and tirelessly patrol the digital borders for intruders. Regular testing through simulations serves as a litmus test, ensuring your plan is finely tuned and ready to deploy.

In Conclusion: Your Cybersecurity Citadel

With incident response planning and management, you can construct a resilient fortress in the face of cybersecurity onslaughts. In other words, this process equips you with the tools to face adversity head on, showcasing your unwavering dedication to business goals, objectives, mission, and stakeholders. Every step—from identification to containment, analysis to recovery—molds this digital stronghold. Remember that incident response isn't just a strategy; it's a testament to your adaptability and resilience in the face of digital storms.

Chapter 5:
Continuous Monitoring and Threat Intelligence

In the realm of modern business, where digital landscapes span the horizon, the guards posted at the gates of your virtual fortress must be vigilant, well informed, and prepared for the unforeseen. This chapter delves into the pivotal role of continuous monitoring and strategic threat intelligence within the intricate tapestry of cybersecurity and why they're profoundly significant for you as a business leader.

The Sentinel's Vigilance: Continuous Monitoring

Imagine a virtual sentinel stationed at every gateway and passage within your digital dominion, equipped with unerring senses to detect even the faintest signs of intrusion. This is the essence of continuous monitoring. In this age of relentless cyberthreats, an enterprise's network, systems, and data require constant surveillance. This entails the judicious use of state-of-the-art security technologies such as intrusion detection and prevention systems, firewalls, and the sophisticated orchestration of security information and event management systems.

Continuous monitoring serves as the heartbeat of a business's cybersecurity strategy, capable of issuing timely alerts to its expert guardians whenever there is a whisper of unauthorized access, malware contamination, or audacious intrusion attempts. It's akin to an impregnable fortress whose very walls are sentient, sensing and repelling threats in real time.

Infiltrating the Adversary's Mind: Strategic Threat Intelligence

Yet to truly fortify your digital assets, you must endeavor to understand the minds of those who would assail your online presence. Enter strategic threat intelligence, similar to a network of spies, collecting and deciphering intelligence about potential adversaries and their motivations; tactics, techniques, and procedures; and capabilities.

Think of threat intelligence as the clandestine conversations that analysts eavesdrop on, revealing the strategies that adversaries and threat actors might employ. This depth of knowledge equips leaders not only to preempt attacks but also to develop counter strategies that outwit even the most cunning opponents. Just as a chess grandmaster anticipates rival moves, business leaders must anticipate threats before they materialize.

Forging an Alliance of Insight: Integrated Vigilance and Response

The true power of continuous monitoring and strategic threat intelligence is unveiled when they unite seamlessly. The melding of these two pillars forms an impervious bulwark against cyber assailants.

Sources of threat intelligence, derived from open-source intelligence, commercial threat intelligence feeds, and collaborations with other organizations and governmental agencies, provide you with a comprehensive mosaic of potential threats. This mosaic is interwoven with the real-time insights gained through continuous monitoring.

Within the incident response procedures lies the final bastion of defense. As mentioned, your incident response team, similar to troops swiftly deployed in times of crisis, is adeptly trained, guided by meticulously documented procedures, and well versed in the orchestration of your battle-tested incident response plan. The synergy between continuous monitoring and strategic threat intelligence ensures that potential breaches are detected, analyzed, and neutralized with the utmost efficiency.

Conclusion: A Shield Unyielding

In closing, continuous monitoring and strategic threat intelligence are crucial to implementing a digital stronghold. Continuous monitoring, driven by cutting-edge technologies, shields organizations from threats as they emerge, and strategic threat intelligence understands the minds of those who would undermine defenses. The bond between these two elements, solidified within solid incident response procedures, ensures that the fortress remains unyielding in the face of adversity.

In the next chapter, we will unveil the critical role of educating and raising awareness among employees in our grand cybersecurity narrative. Until then, let us stride forward with the lessons learned here: that defenses, combined with continuous vigilance and insightful intelligence, are paramount assets.

Chapter 6:
Secure Cloud Computing

As organizations increasingly rely on cloud computing for their data storage and processing needs, ensuring the security of cloud environments becomes paramount. This chapter explores the complexities and challenges of secure cloud computing, providing insights into the best practices and strategies for safeguarding data in the digital age. By understanding the importance of security measures, enterprises can navigate the evolving threat landscape and leverage the benefits of cloud computing with confidence. Secure cloud computing has emerged as a crucial component of enterprise infrastructure, offering scalable, cost-effective, and flexible solutions for managing data and applications.

The Evolution of Cloud Computing

The concept of cloud computing can be traced back to the 1960s, when computer scientist J. C. R. Licklider envisioned an interconnected computer network that would allow users to access data and programs remotely. This idea laid the foundation for the development of ARPANET, the precursor to the internet. Over the next few decades, advancements in networking, virtualization, and distributed computing paved the way for the emergence of cloud computing as we know it today.

In the late 1990s and early 2000s, the groundwork for cloud computing was laid with the introduction of Software as a Service (SaaS), Platform as a Service (PaaS), and Infrastructure as a Service (IaaS) models. Salesforce.com, founded in 1999, was one of the pioneers of the SaaS model, offering web-based customer relationship management software. Meanwhile, companies like Amazon Web Services (AWS) and Google launched IaaS and PaaS offerings, providing developers with scalable infrastructure and platforms to build and deploy applications.

The mid-2000s witnessed the emergence of major public cloud providers that revolutionized the cloud computing landscape. AWS, launched in 2006, became a game changer by offering a wide range of cloud services, including storage, computing power, and databases, on a pay-as-you-go basis. This scalability and flexibility attracted businesses of all sizes, enabling them to offload infrastructure management and focus on core competencies. Other tech giants, such as Microsoft with Azure and Google with Google Cloud Platform, followed suit, intensifying competition and driving innovation in the cloud market.

As organizations embraced cloud computing, they began to realize the need for a more flexible and diversified approach. This led to the rise of hybrid and multicloud environments. Hybrid cloud combines public and private clouds, allowing businesses to leverage the benefits of both while meeting specific security, compliance, or performance requirements. Multicloud, on the other hand, involves using multiple cloud providers to distribute workloads and reduce vendor lock-in. These approaches provide businesses with greater agility and resilience and the ability to choose the best-fit solutions for their specific needs. Cloud computing has had a profound effect on industries across the board. In the retail sector, companies such as Amazon have leveraged cloud infrastructure to power their e-commerce platforms and enable global scalability. The entertainment industry has embraced cloud-based streaming services such as Netflix and Spotify, providing users with on-demand access to a vast library of content. Health-care organizations are using cloud solutions for secure data storage, telemedicine, and collaborative research. Similarly, the financial sector is adopting cloud computing to enhance data analysis, risk management, and customer experience.

The evolution of cloud computing has also given rise to cloud-native technologies and practices. Containers such as Docker and orchestration platforms such as Kubernetes have enabled efficient application deployment and management across different cloud environments. Serverless computing, represented by services such as AWS Lambda and Google Cloud Functions, allows developers to focus solely on writing code without worrying about server management. These advancements have further accelerated the adoption of cloud computing and empowered organizations to build scalable and resilient applications.

The future of cloud computing holds immense promise. As technology continues to advance, we can expect further improvements in areas such as edge computing, artificial intelligence, and quantum computing. Edge computing brings the power of cloud computing closer to the end users, reducing latency and enabling real-time data processing. AI and machine learning capabilities integrated into cloud platforms will enhance data analytics, automation, and personalized experiences. Quantum computing, although still in its early stages, has the potential to revolutionize computational power and solve complex problems at an unprecedented scale.

The evolution of cloud computing has been nothing short of transformative. From its humble beginnings as a concept to the emergence of major public cloud providers, cloud computing has reshaped industries, empowered businesses, and unleashed a new era of innovation. The flexibility, scalability, and cost-efficiency of cloud computing have made it an integral part of the digital infrastructure.

Understanding Cloud Security Risks

As organizations increasingly adopt cloud computing services, understanding and mitigating cloud security risks have become paramount. Cloud technology offers numerous benefits, including scalability, flexibility, and cost-efficiency, but it also introduces unique security challenges. This section explores the various risks associated with cloud computing and provides insights into effective security measures. By gaining a comprehensive understanding of these risks, businesses can implement robust security strategies to safeguard their sensitive data and maintain the trust of their stakeholders.

One of the primary concerns in cloud computing is the risk of data breaches and unauthorized access. Storing data in the cloud means entrusting it to a third-party service provider, increasing the potential for unauthorized access by malicious actors. Breaches can occur because of weak authentication mechanisms, poor access controls, or vulnerabilities in the cloud infrastructure. These breaches can result in sensitive data leaks, financial losses, reputational damage, and legal consequences. For example, in 2019, Capital One experienced a significant data breach in which over one hundred million customer records were compromised because of a misconfigured firewall in their cloud infrastructure.

Effective identity and access management (IAM) is crucial in ensuring the security of cloud resources. However, misconfigured IAM policies or weak authentication mechanisms can lead to unauthorized access and data exposure. Insufficient access controls can result in unauthorized users' gaining privileged access to critical systems and data. A notable example is the 2017 "Verizon Data Breach Investigations Report," which revealed that compromised credentials were a leading cause of data breaches. Implementing strong authentication protocols and multifactor authentication and regularly reviewing and updating access privileges are essential to mitigating this risk. Although cloud service providers implement robust backup and disaster recovery mechanisms, data loss remains a concern. Data can be lost because of hardware failures, software glitches, natural disasters, or human errors. Inadequate backup strategies or failure to encrypt sensitive data can result in permanent data loss or the exposure of confidential information. A well-known example is the 2017 incident in which GitLab, a code-hosting platform, suffered data loss due to human error during a database replication process. Implementing data-backup and recovery procedures, including regular backups, offsite storage, and encryption, is crucial to mitigate this risk.

Insider threats pose a significant risk to cloud security, as authorized users with privileged access can intentionally or unintentionally compromise data. These threats may arise from disgruntled employees, contractors, or partners with access to sensitive information. Insiders can misuse their privileges, leak data, or cause disruptions to cloud services. One example is the 2019 incident involving a former employee of Tesla who allegedly accessed confidential company data and shared it with third parties. Implementing strict access controls, monitoring user activities, and conducting regular security awareness training are essential to mitigate insider threats.

Cloud computing introduces complex compliance and legal considerations. Different industries and regions have specific regulatory requirements regarding data privacy, security, and storage. Organizations must ensure that their chosen cloud service provider complies with relevant regulations, such as the General Data Protection Regulation (GDPR) or the Health Insurance Portability and Accountability Act (HIPAA). Failure to meet compliance requirements can lead to hefty fines, reputational damage, and legal consequences. For instance, in 2020, a European retailer faced GDPR fines of €35 million for a data breach that exposed customer information. Conducting thorough due diligence on cloud service providers, ensuring that contractual agreements include compliance obligations, and regularly assessing compliance are vital in addressing this risk. Cloud service providers are not immune to vulnerabilities. The security of an enterprise's data depends on the security practices and infrastructure of the chosen cloud provider. If the provider experiences a security breach or fails to address vulnerabilities promptly, it can have severe consequences for customer data. A prominent example is the 2020 Microsoft Exchange Server breach, in which attackers exploited vulnerabilities in the on-premises email server software, affecting numerous organizations' data security. Conducting thorough assessments of a cloud service provider's security practices, certifications, and incident response procedures is crucial in mitigating risks of this nature to your business's data.

Understanding the risks associated with cloud computing is vital for organizations seeking to leverage its benefits while maintaining data security. Data breaches, inadequate identity and access management, data loss, insider threats, compliance issues, and vulnerabilities in cloud service providers are among the significant risks that must be addressed. By implementing robust security measures such as strong authentication protocols, encryption, backup and recovery strategies, strict access controls, and thorough due diligence of cloud service providers, organizations can enhance their cloud security posture. Ultimately, a proactive approach to cloud security enables businesses to protect sensitive data, maintain customer trust, and stay resilient in the digital era.

Essential Security Measures for Cloud Computing

As cloud computing continues to reshape the business landscape, ensuring robust security measures is crucial to protect sensitive data and maintain the trust of users. Although cloud technology offers numerous benefits, it also introduces unique security challenges. This section explores essential security measures for cloud computing, focusing on key areas such as data encryption, access controls, vulnerability management, and incident response. By implementing these measures, organizations can enhance the security of their cloud environments and mitigate the risks associated with storing and processing data in the cloud.

Data encryption is a fundamental security measure in cloud computing. Encrypting data ensures that even if it is intercepted or accessed without authorization, it remains unreadable and unusable. Organizations should adopt strong encryption algorithms to protect data both in transit and at rest within the cloud infrastructure. Encryption keys should be carefully managed and stored separately from the encrypted data to maintain the integrity of the encryption process. By encrypting sensitive data, organizations can add an additional layer of protection against unauthorized access.

Effective access controls are critical to preventing unauthorized access to cloud resources. Organizations should implement robust identity and access management practices to ensure that only authorized individuals can access and modify data stored in the cloud. This includes implementing strong authentication mechanisms such as requiring multifactor authentication and enforcing the principle of least privilege, granting users only the necessary access rights for their roles. Regularly reviewing and updating access privileges and promptly revoking access for employees who leave the organization are essential to maintaining a secure access control framework.

Regularly assessing and addressing vulnerabilities in cloud environments is essential to prevent potential security breaches. Organizations should establish a robust vulnerability management program that includes continuous monitoring and vulnerability scanning and timely patching of software and systems. By staying vigilant and promptly addressing identified vulnerabilities, organizations can minimize the risk of exploitation by malicious actors. Regular vulnerability assessments and penetration testing can provide valuable insights into the security posture of the cloud infrastructure and help identify and remediate potential weaknesses.

Having a well-defined incident response plan is crucial in cloud computing to effectively respond to security incidents. Organizations should establish clear procedures for detecting, responding to, and recovering from security breaches or unauthorized access. This includes establishing incident response teams, defining roles and responsibilities, and implementing incident monitoring and detection tools. Regularly testing the incident response plan through simulated exercises can help identify areas for improvement and ensure a swift and effective response in case of a real security incident. Continuous security monitoring and logging are vital to detect and respond to potential security threats in a cloud environment. Organizations should implement robust logging mechanisms to capture and store relevant security events, including authentication attempts, access requests, and system changes. Security information and event management solutions can provide centralized log management and real-time analysis of security events, enabling timely detection of suspicious activities. By monitoring and analyzing security logs, organizations can proactively identify and respond to security incidents.

Securing cloud computing environments requires a comprehensive approach that addresses data encryption, access controls, vulnerability management, incident response, and security monitoring. By implementing these essential security measures, organizations can enhance the security of their cloud infrastructure and protect sensitive data from unauthorized access and data breaches. As cloud computing continues to evolve, organizations must stay vigilant, regularly assess their security measures, and adapt to emerging threats to ensure the integrity and confidentiality of their data in the cloud.

Compliance and Legal Considerations

As organizations increasingly adopt cloud computing, they must navigate a complex landscape of compliance and legal considerations to ensure the security and privacy of their data. This section explores the key compliance requirements and legal considerations that organizations must address when implementing secure cloud computing solutions. It discusses the importance of regulatory compliance, data privacy laws, industry-specific regulations, and contractual agreements with cloud service providers. By understanding and adhering to these compliance and legal requirements, organizations can build a robust and legally sound cloud security framework.

Compliance with applicable regulations is crucial for organizations operating in various industries. Depending on the geographic location and industry sector, organizations may need to comply with regulations such as the General Data Protection Regulation (GDPR) in the European Union, HIPAA in the health-care industry, or the Payment Card Industry Data Security Standard (PCI DSS) for organizations handling payment card data. It is essential for organizations to understand the specific compliance requirements relevant to their operations and ensure that their cloud computing practices align with these regulations. For example, the GDPR, which came into effect in May 2018 requires organizations that handle personal data of EU residents to implement strong security measures, including encryption and data breach notification protocols. Noncompliance with the GDPR can result in significant fines and reputational damage.

Data privacy is a critical aspect of secure cloud computing. Organizations must ensure that personal and sensitive data stored or processed in the cloud is protected in accordance with applicable data protection laws. This includes obtaining necessary consent for data processing, implementing appropriate security controls, and ensuring that data subject rights are respected. Privacy laws, such as the California Consumer Privacy Act (CCPA) and Brazil's General Data Protection Law, impose strict requirements on the handling of personal data, including cross-border data transfers. In 2020, the Court of Justice of the European Union invalidated the privacy shield framework, which had allowed the transfer of personal data between the EU and the United States. This decision highlighted the importance of ensuring that cross-border data transfers comply with relevant data protection regulations.

Certain industries have specific regulations and standards that organizations must adhere to when using cloud computing. For example, the financial sector must comply with regulations such as the Sarbanes-Oxley Act and the Basel III framework. Health-care organizations must adhere to HIPAA regulations, and government agencies must comply with frameworks such as the Federal Risk and Authorization Management Program. Organizations operating in these sectors must ensure that their cloud computing practices meet the unique requirements set forth by these industry-specific regulations. The financial industry is subject to stringent regulations to ensure the integrity and security of financial data. Cloud service providers catering to the financial sector often undergo independent audits and certifications to demonstrate compliance with industry-specific standards such as the Payment Card Industry Data Security Standard (PCI DSS).

When adopting cloud computing services, organizations must establish strong contractual agreements with cloud service providers to ensure that security and privacy requirements are met. These agreements should address key aspects such as data ownership, data breach notification, service-level agreements, security controls, and the right to audit the cloud provider's security practices. Organizations must carefully review and negotiate these agreements to ensure that their specific security and compliance needs are adequately addressed. In 2020, the European Data Protection Board published recommendations for organizations when using cloud services. These recommendations emphasized the need for organizations to assess the contractual terms with cloud providers, including data protection obligations, data location, subprocessing arrangements, and audit rights.

Compliance and legal considerations play a pivotal role in secure cloud computing. Organizations must understand and adhere to relevant regulations, industry-specific requirements, and contractual agreements to ensure the security and privacy of their data in the cloud. By actively addressing compliance and legal considerations, organizations can mitigate the risks associated with data breaches, regulatory fines, and reputational damage. It is crucial to establish a robust governance framework that includes regular assessments, audits, and updates to maintain compliance with evolving regulations and best practices in secure cloud computing.

Emerging Technologies for Cloud Security

As cloud computing continues to evolve, new technologies are emerging to enhance the security of cloud environments. This section explores some of the key emerging technologies that are revolutionizing cloud security. These technologies address the challenges posed by evolving threats, data breaches, and the need for stronger security controls. By leveraging these innovative solutions, organizations can enhance the security posture of their cloud infrastructure and protect their valuable data assets.

Machine learning (ML) and AI technologies are playing a crucial role in bolstering cloud security. ML and AI algorithms can analyze vast amounts of data and identify patterns that indicate potential security threats. These technologies can detect anomalies, predict attacks, and automate incident response, enabling organizations to respond to threats in real time. ML- and AI-based solutions also help improve authentication mechanisms, user-behavior analytics, and threat intelligence, making cloud environments more secure and resilient. Google Cloud uses ML and AI technologies in its Cloud Security Command Center. It uses advanced analytics to identify and prioritize security risks across cloud assets, providing organizations with actionable insights to enhance their security posture.

Blockchain technology, which gained prominence with cryptocurrencies such as Bitcoin, is finding applications in cloud security. Blockchain provides a decentralized and immutable ledger that enhances the integrity and transparency of data stored in the cloud. It can be used for secure identity management, ensuring that only authorized users can access cloud resources. Additionally, blockchain can facilitate secure and auditable data sharing among multiple parties, reducing the risks associated with data tampering and unauthorized access. IBM is leveraging blockchain technology for secure cloud storage. By using blockchain-based encryption and distributed ledger technology, IBM Cloud Object Storage ensures the confidentiality, integrity, and availability of data stored in the cloud.

Software-defined security (SDS) is an emerging approach that enables organizations to abstract and centralize security controls in cloud environments. SDS separates the security policies and mechanisms from the underlying infrastructure, allowing for more flexibility and scalability. With SDS, security policies can be dynamically applied to workloads and data, ensuring consistent protection across the cloud infrastructure. This approach also enables automation and orchestration of security tasks, simplifying security management and reducing the risk of misconfigurations. VMware's NSX platform is a leading example of SDS for cloud security. It provides a virtualized network security solution that enables organizations to define and enforce security policies for their cloud workloads, regardless of the underlying infrastructure.

Zero-trust architecture (ZTA) is an emerging security framework that assumes no implicit trust, even for users and devices within the network perimeter. ZTA focuses on verifying and validating every access request, regardless of the user's location or device. It employs techniques such as multifactor authentication, microsegmentation, and continuous monitoring to ensure that only authorized entities gain access to cloud resources. By adopting a zero-trust approach, organizations can strengthen their cloud security posture and mitigate the risk of unauthorized access and data breaches. Google Cloud's BeyondCorp model is based on the zero-trust principle. It replaces traditional perimeter-based security with context-aware access policies, strong authentication, and continuous monitoring to protect cloud resources from internal and external threats.

Emerging technologies are reshaping the landscape of cloud security, providing innovative solutions to combat evolving threats and protect sensitive data. Machine learning and artificial intelligence enhance threat detection and response capabilities, and blockchain technology ensures data integrity and secure sharing. Software-defined security enables flexible and scalable security controls, and ZTA enhances access control mechanisms. By embracing these emerging technologies, organizations can bolster their cloud security posture and stay ahead of the ever-changing threat landscape, safeguarding their valuable assets in the cloud.

Building a Culture of Cloud Security

Ensuring robust security practices within an organization's cloud environment goes beyond implementing technical solutions. It requires fostering a culture of cloud security in which every individual understands their role in safeguarding sensitive data and follows best practices.

This section explores the key components of building a culture of cloud security within an organization, emphasizing the importance of education, training, and continuous improvement.

Building a culture of cloud security begins with educating employees about the potential risks and best practices associated with cloud computing. This includes creating awareness about the types of threats, such as data breaches, unauthorized access, and social engineering attacks. Employees should be educated about the importance of using strong passwords, enabling multifactor authentication, and being cautious of phishing attempts. Regular training sessions, workshops, and awareness campaigns can help instill a security mindset within the organization. Netflix has a comprehensive security awareness program that educates employees about the importance of data protection and the role they play in maintaining security. They provide ongoing training and simulations to raise awareness and promote a security-conscious culture. Establishing clear and comprehensive security policies and procedures is vital for building a culture of cloud security. These policies should outline the acceptable use of cloud resources, data classification and handling, incident response protocols, and employee responsibilities. Employees should be familiar with these policies and trained in how to comply with them. Regular updates and communication about policy changes or new security guidelines ensure that employees stay informed and aligned with the organization's security objectives. Google has a robust security policy framework that governs its cloud services. The policies define data protection measures, access controls, and incident response protocols, ensuring a secure cloud environment. Regular audits and assessments help ensure policy adherence.

Creating a culture of cloud security involves fostering a sense of responsibility and accountability among employees. Individuals should understand that they play active roles in protecting sensitive data and maintaining the security of the organization's cloud resources. Encouraging employees to report any suspicious activities, vulnerabilities, or potential security risks creates a collaborative and proactive security culture. Regular security assessments and audits can also help organizations assess employee compliance and identify areas for improvement. Microsoft has a "see something, say something" approach to security, encouraging employees to report any potential security concerns promptly. This fosters a culture of accountability and empowers individuals to contribute to the overall security posture.

Building a culture of cloud security requires a commitment to continuous improvement and adaptation. As threats evolve and new technologies emerge, organizations must stay vigilant and update their security practices accordingly. Regular training sessions, security awareness programs, and knowledge-sharing initiatives can keep employees informed about the latest security trends and best practices. Conducting post-incident reviews and implementing lessons learned help drive continuous improvement and ensure that security measures align with evolving threats. AWS encourages a culture of continuous improvement through its "shared responsibility" model. They provide regular security updates, guidelines, and best practices to help organizations adapt their security measures based on the changing threat landscape. Building a culture of cloud security is essential for organizations to effectively protect their sensitive data and maintain a secure cloud environment. Education and awareness programs, clear policies, employee accountability, and a commitment to continuous improvement are key components of this culture. By fostering a security-conscious mindset and empowering employees to actively contribute to cloud security, organizations can mitigate risks, strengthen their security posture, and ensure the confidentiality, integrity, and availability of their data in the cloud.

Conclusion

In summary, secure cloud computing plays a crucial role in protecting organizational data in the digital age. It is vitally important for organizations to stay abreast of evolving security threats, implement comprehensive security measures, and foster a culture of security within enterprises. By adopting a holistic approach to cloud security, organizations can mitigate risks, enhance data protection, and leverage the full potential of cloud computing while maintaining the trust of their customers and stakeholders.

Chapter 7:
Risk Assessment
A Comprehensive Exploration of Its Significance and Process

Risk assessment is a crucial aspect of contemporary decision-making across various domains, from business and finance to healthcare and technology. It's a systematic process that enables organizations and individuals to identify, evaluate, and manage potential risks, ensuring informed choices that balance potential gains and losses. By understanding the concept, process, benefits, and challenges of risk assessment, we can navigate uncertainties with greater confidence and precision.

In a world marked by rapid change, uncertainty has become a constant companion. From the boardrooms of multinational corporations to the decisions made by individuals, the significance of understanding, evaluating, and managing risks cannot be overstated.

This is where risk assessment steps in as a pivotal tool for navigating uncertainties and making informed choices that shape the trajectory of organizations and lives. Through a comprehensive exploration of the importance of risk assessment, this chapter delves into how it provides a structured framework for identifying potential hazards, analyzing their consequences, and implementing strategies to mitigate those consequences.

At its core, risk assessment is a structured process designed to evaluate potential risks associated with a specific course of action, decision, or situation. It embodies a holistic approach that systematically identifies uncertainties, quantifies their potential effects, and assists decision-makers in crafting strategies that mitigate potential negative outcomes. By providing a methodical examination of uncertainties, risk assessment enables individuals and organizations to allocate resources more effectively, bolster resilience, and make well-informed choices.

Risk assessment is a multistep journey that translates uncertainties into actionable insights. The first step is to identify potential risks that could influence an organization's objectives. These risks can range from operational and financial challenges to legal and reputational issues. The identification phase lays the groundwork for a comprehensive assessment. Once identified, risks are subjected to thorough analysis. This step involves evaluating the probability of a risk materializing and estimating its potential consequences. This quantification of risks facilitates a clearer understanding of their potential effects on objectives. The evaluation phase involves comparing the analyzed risks against predetermined criteria or thresholds. Risks that exceed these thresholds might be deemed unacceptable and necessitate immediate attention. This evaluation provides the basis for prioritizing risk management efforts.

Based on the evaluation, organizations can chart a path for risk treatment. This involves determining strategies for managing risks, such as risk avoidance, risk mitigation, risk transfer, or risk acceptance. For instance, an aviation company might choose to mitigate the risk of engine failure by implementing rigorous maintenance procedures. The journey of risk assessment doesn't conclude with risk treatment. Ongoing monitoring and periodic review are essential to accommodate changing circumstances, emerging risks, and the effectiveness of risk management strategies.

The importance of risk assessment extends across industries and sectors, profoundly affecting decision-making. Risk assessment equips decision-makers with essential information needed to make well-founded choices. It empowers them to weigh potential rewards against potential risks, leading to more prudent decisions.

In industries governed by stringent regulations, risk assessment aids organizations in identifying gaps and taking proactive measures to meet regulatory mandates. This not only ensures compliance but also safeguards the organization's reputation. Risk assessment guides organizations in judiciously allocating resources, which are finite. By focusing on high-impact risks, organizations optimize their efforts to manage potential threats effectively. Far from stifling innovation, risk assessment fuels it. By identifying and managing risks associated with novel ventures, technologies, or products, organizations can navigate challenges and foster successful innovation. Transparent risk assessment processes foster stakeholder trust. Shareholders, customers, and partners are more likely to place their faith in organizations that demonstrate a comprehensive understanding of risks and a commitment to managing them prudently.

The merits of risk assessment are evident, but challenges are inherent. Accurate risk assessment hinges on reliable data. Organizations often grapple with gathering comprehensive and up-to-date data on risks. Furthermore, ensuring data quality is paramount to producing accurate risk analyses. Assessing risks introduces an element of subjectivity. Different individuals might interpret risks differently, potentially affecting the accuracy and consistency of the assessment. Risks seldom exist in isolation; they often interact in complex webs. Capturing these interdependencies is challenging but essential for accurate risk assessment. In a rapidly evolving landscape, new risks can emerge unexpectedly. Anticipating these risks and assessing their potential effects requires agility and foresight. Risk assessment involves predicting the likelihood and consequences of future events—an inherently uncertain task.

Organizations can adopt a variety of strategies to overcome these challenges:

- Invest in robust data management systems to ensure data availability, accuracy, and reliability.

- Employ automation and advanced analytics to assist in data aggregation, analysis, and visualization.

- Encourage cross-functional collaboration during risk assessment.

- Involve diverse perspectives to enrich risk identification and analysis.

- Ensure transparency in the risk assessment process.

- Clearly communicate the methods, assumptions, and data sources used in risk assessment.

- Strive for transparency to enhance credibility and stakeholder trust.

- Recognize the interconnected nature of risks and develop scenarios that capture potential interdependencies.

- Use scenario planning for assistance in anticipating and preparing for ripple effects.

- Foster a culture of continuous learning and improvement.

- Regularly update risk assessment methodologies based on lessons learned to enhance accuracy.

- Invest in building risk assessment expertise within the organization.

- Consult trained professionals for assistance in navigating complexities and making more accurate judgments.

Risk assessment is a bedrock for well-informed decisions across diverse realms. By identifying, evaluating, and managing potential risks, organizations optimize resource allocation, drive innovation, and maintain stakeholder trust. Although challenges exist, effective data management, collaboration, transparency, scenario planning, continuous learning, and expertise development provide avenues for overcoming them. As humanity navigates a world of uncertainties, risk assessment empowers individuals and organizations alike to tread with assurance, guided by strategic insight and precision. It provides a structured approach to identifying, analyzing, and managing potential risks that organizations may encounter. Delving into its intricate steps offers a comprehensive overview of the risk assessment process, underscoring its significance in steering organizations toward informed and resilient choices.

1. Risk Identification

The initial step in risk assessment involves identifying potential risks that could affect an organization's objectives. This entails a systematic exploration of various internal and external factors that could pose threats. These risks can stem from a myriad of sources, such as operational vulnerabilities, changes in market dynamics, regulatory shifts, technological disruptions, or unforeseen events. Engaging stakeholders across different levels of the organization facilitates a comprehensive inventory of potential risks, laying the foundation for further analysis.

2. Risk Categorization

Once potential risks are identified, they are categorized based on shared characteristics or attributes. This categorization aids in streamlining the assessment process, allowing organizations to apply specific methodologies tailored to each risk category. Risks are often grouped into distinct classes, such as operational, financial, reputational, compliance-related, or strategic risks. By organizing risks into coherent clusters, organizations are better equipped to allocate resources and prioritize their assessment efforts.

3. Risk Assessment

The assessment phase involves evaluating identified risks to understand their likelihood of occurrence and potential effects on organizational objectives. This process employs both qualitative and quantitative techniques. Qualitative assessment involves expert judgment and consideration of factors such as severity, frequency, and detectability. Quantitative assessment, on the other hand, involves assigning numerical values to risks using historical data, statistical modeling, and predictive analysis. This phase provides organizations with a nuanced comprehension of the potential consequences associated with each risk.

4. Risk Evaluation

Once potential risks are assessed, the next step involves evaluating these risks against predefined criteria or thresholds. This evaluation assesses whether the risks are within the organization's risk appetite and tolerance levels. Risks that exceed these thresholds are deemed unacceptable and warrant immediate attention. Risk evaluation plays a critical role in prioritizing risk management efforts, ensuring that resources are allocated to address high-impact risks that could disrupt organizational objectives.

5. Risk Treatment

Following risk evaluation, organizations proceed to the risk treatment phase, during which strategies are formulated to manage and mitigate identified risks. Risk treatment options are determined by the nature of the risk and the organization's risk appetite. Strategies include risk avoidance, which eliminates the risk by altering processes or decisions; risk mitigation to reduce the likelihood or consequences of the risk; risk transfer, which outsources the risk to third parties; or risk acceptance—the organization consciously decides to tolerate the risk. The chosen strategy aligns with the organization's objectives and considers cost-effectiveness.

6. Implementation and Monitoring

Once risk treatment strategies are defined, the implementation phase commences. This involves executing the strategies outlined to manage and mitigate identified risks. Cross-functional collaboration, resource allocation, and adherence to established timelines are essential components of this phase. Simultaneously, monitoring and continuous assessment are pivotal in ensuring the effectiveness of the chosen strategies. Regularly tracking the progress of risk treatment initiatives, analyzing emerging threats, and reviewing the applicability of strategies in evolving scenarios is critical to maintaining robust risk management practices.

7. Communication and Reporting

Transparency is central to risk assessment and management. Organizations are tasked with communicating the outcomes of risk assessment to stakeholders, ranging from internal teams and senior leadership to external stakeholders such as regulators, customers, and investors. Comprehensive reporting ensures that stakeholders are aware of the organization's risk profile, the strategies employed to address risks, and the progress made in managing uncertainties. Effective communication builds accountability, stakeholder confidence, and external alignment.

8. Continuous Improvement

The risk assessment process is iterative, acknowledging that risks evolve over time. Organizations are tasked with a commitment to continuous improvement. This involves refining risk assessment methodologies and strategies based on lessons learned, emerging risks, and changing circumstances. By fostering a culture of learning, organizations ensure that their risk management practices remain agile, adaptable, and relevant in the face of dynamic uncertainties.

In conclusion, risk assessment transcends its process-oriented nature to become a strategic imperative for organizations navigating today's intricate business environment. By following the structured steps of identification, categorization, assessment, evaluation, treatment, implementation, monitoring, communication, and continuous improvement, organizations enhance their capacity to make well-informed decisions and cultivate resilience in the face of uncertainties. This process not only fosters proactive risk management but also reinforces organizational agility and the ability to seize opportunities while safeguarding objectives and stakeholder interests.

In the dynamic landscape of modern business, the practice of risk assessment has emerged as a fundamental pillar for informed decision-making and proactive management. The business environment is rife with uncertainties ranging from technological disruptions and market shifts to regulatory changes and unforeseen events. In this context, the significance of conducting comprehensive risk assessments cannot be overstated. The next section delves into the myriad reasons why risk assessment should be an integral part of an organization's strategic toolkit, underscoring the value it brings to the table in terms of informed decision-making, resource optimization, regulatory compliance, stakeholder trust, and resilience against uncertainties.

Informed Decision-Making: The Guiding Light of Risk Assessment

At the heart of every business decision lies the goal of optimizing outcomes while minimizing potential setbacks. Herein lies the essence of risk assessment. By systematically identifying and analyzing potential risks, organizations gain valuable insights into the factors that could affect their objectives. This understanding allows decision-makers to weigh potential rewards against potential risks and make choices that align with their overall strategy. Risk assessments provide the requisite data and context to make well-informed decisions, thereby steering organizations away from hasty choices that could lead to unfavorable outcomes.

Resource Optimization: Deploying Assets Strategically

Resources, whether financial, human, or technological, are finite and precious commodities. Risk assessments help people and organizations allocate them judiciously. By identifying potential risks, organizations can allocate resources in a manner that optimally addresses these vulnerabilities. High-impact risks can be prioritized, ensuring that a disproportionate amount of resources is dedicated to managing them. This strategic allocation enhances efficiency, as resources are channeled toward minimizing risks that could potentially have a substantial effect on organizational objectives.

Regulatory Compliance: Navigating a Complex Landscape

In an era of stringent regulations, compliance is not merely an option but a prerequisite for sustainable business operations. Risk assessments play a pivotal role in this regard. They identify potential compliance breaches and vulnerabilities, allowing organizations to rectify issues before they escalate. With the labyrinthine web of regulations governing different industries, risk assessments provide clarity and direction, ensuring that organizations stay abreast of legal requirements and avoid costly penalties.

Stakeholder Trust: The Bedrock of Relationships

Stakeholders, whether they are investors, customers, partners, or employees, place their trust in organizations to act in their best interests. This trust is built on transparency, accountability, and the ability to manage uncertainties effectively. Risk assessments contribute significantly to this foundation. By demonstrating a proactive approach to identifying and managing potential risks, organizations bolster stakeholder confidence. This transparency fosters trust and reassures stakeholders that their interests are paramount.

Resilience against Uncertainties: Weathering the Storm

The business landscape is replete with unforeseen events that can disrupt even the best-laid plans. Risk assessments serve as a shield against such uncertainties. By identifying potential risks, organizations can devise strategies to mitigate their consequences. This proactive stance ensures that organizations are better prepared to weather unexpected challenges. The ability to navigate uncertainties is integral to organizational resilience and longevity, and risk assessments provide the road map for this preparedness.

Optimal Use of Opportunities: Seizing the Moment

Risk and reward are two sides of the same coin. Opportunities, like risks, are inherent in the business environment. Risk assessments not only identify potential pitfalls but also equip organizations to evaluate the risks associated with potential opportunities. This enables organizations to make calculated choices, ensuring that the pursuit of opportunities is balanced against potential drawbacks. Risk assessments thus empower organizations to seize the right opportunities while minimizing associated risks.

Enhanced Innovation: Navigating the Frontier of Creativity

Innovation, the lifeblood of progress, is often fraught with uncertainties. Risk assessments offer a structured framework to manage the risks inherent in innovation. By identifying potential barriers, pitfalls, and vulnerabilities, organizations can navigate the path of innovation more strategically. This encourages a culture of experimentation, as decision-makers have a clear understanding of the risks involved and can take calculated steps toward driving innovation without endangering the organization's stability.

Operational Efficiency: Streamlining Processes

Operational inefficiencies can stem from a variety of sources, including unidentified risks. Risk assessments shed light on these potential inefficiencies by highlighting areas of vulnerability. This insight allows organizations to streamline processes, identify redundancies, and allocate resources more efficiently. Operational excellence is closely tied to the ability to anticipate and manage risks that could disrupt the smooth functioning of an organization.

Holistic Approach to Governance: Embracing Comprehensive Risk Management

Effective governance extends beyond financial prudence. It involves a holistic understanding of an organization's risk profile. Risk assessments provide the panoramic view required for comprehensive governance. They help decision-makers understand the interplay of risks, enabling them to make choices that account for potential ripple effects. This holistic approach ensures that governance strategies are robust and inclusive of all potential vulnerabilities.

Cultivating a Culture of Resilience: From Individuals to Organizations

A culture of resilience starts with individuals who understand the importance of risk management. Risk assessments cascade this understanding from the leadership to every level of the organization. When employees are cognizant of potential risks and of their role in mitigating those risks, a culture of responsibility and accountability is nurtured. This collective mindset fortifies the organization's ability to anticipate and navigate uncertainties.

In conclusion, risk assessments are not a mere checkbox on the organizational to-do list; they are a strategic imperative that equips organizations to navigate the complexities of a dynamic environment by offering insights for informed decision-making, optimizing resource allocation, ensuring regulatory compliance, and fostering stakeholder trust.

Risk assessment, in the realm of modern business, is a pivotal practice that confers an array of invaluable benefits upon organizations of all sizes and sectors. Central to the essence of risk assessment is its role as a beacon for informed decision-making. In the intricate web of business operations, choices are often laden with uncertainties. Risk assessments lay bare potential pitfalls, offering decision-makers a panoramic view of the possible challenges and disruptions that could arise. Armed with this insight, organizations can weigh the potential benefits against the accompanying risks. This informed approach ensures that decisions are not merely reactive but are guided by a strategic understanding of the potential ramifications.

Risk assessments serve as the compass for such allocation. By identifying potential risks that could impede organizational objectives, organizations can allocate resources in a manner that optimally addresses these vulnerabilities. High-impact risks can be prioritized, ensuring that resources are channeled toward managing these risks effectively. This strategic resource allocation enhances efficiency, minimizing wastage and redundancy.

In an age in which regulations are becoming increasingly stringent, compliance is not just a necessity; it's a fundamental requirement for conducting business responsibly. Risk assessments play a pivotal role in this regard. They unearth potential vulnerabilities that could lead to compliance breaches, providing organizations with the insights needed to rectify issues before they escalate. This proactive approach empowers organizations to align their practices with regulatory standards and requirements, averting costly penalties and legal entanglements.

Stakeholders—whether they are investors, customers, partners, or employees—entrust their interests to organizations. This trust hinges on transparency, accountability, and the ability to manage uncertainties adeptly. Risk assessments play a pivotal role in fostering this trust. By demonstrating a proactive approach to identifying and managing potential risks, organizations exhibit their commitment to safeguarding stakeholders' interests. This transparency fosters confidence, reassuring stakeholders that their investments, data, and collaborations are in safe hands.

The ramifications of risk assessments cascade beyond procedural frameworks; they cultivate a culture of resilience within organizations. This collective mindset galvanizes the organization's ability to anticipate and navigate uncertainties. As a result, organizations are better prepared to weather unexpected challenges, sustaining their operations with poise and strategic precision.

As mentioned above, in the dynamic business landscape, opportunities and risks are two sides of the same coin. Just as risk assessments identify potential pitfalls, they also facilitate the evaluation of risks associated with potential opportunities. This empowers organizations to make calculated choices, ensuring that the pursuit of opportunities is balanced against potential drawbacks. By offering insights into the risks associated with opportunities, risk assessments empower organizations to seize the right prospects while minimizing associated uncertainties.

Organizational reputation is delicate and demands constant vigilance. One significant risk event has the potential to tarnish a reputation built over years. Risk assessments serve as a shield against reputation damage. By identifying potential risks that could affect an organization's image, assessments enable organizations to proactively implement strategies to manage and mitigate these risks. This foresight protects the organization's reputation, preserving a valuable asset that is integral to trust and sustained success.

In the absence of risk assessments, resource allocation can be akin to navigating uncharted waters blindfolded. Risk assessments provide the navigational aids needed for prudent resource allocation. They help organizations identify areas of vulnerability that could lead to wastage or inefficiencies. Armed with this insight, organizations can reallocate resources to streamline processes, eliminate redundancies, and optimize operations. This cost-effective approach not only enhances resource utilization but also contributes to the organization's overall financial health.

Crises are not a matter of "if" but "when." Risk assessments play a pivotal role in crisis preparedness. By identifying potential risks that could lead to crises, organizations can develop contingency plans and strategies to manage these risks. This proactive stance empowers organizations to respond swiftly and effectively when crises do arise, minimizing damage and enabling a quicker recovery. Crisis preparedness is a testament to an organization's resilience, and risk assessments provide the blueprint for this readiness.

Individuals who understand the importance of risk management can foster a culture of proactivity and responsibility. Risk assessments cultivate this mindset across all levels of an organization. This collective consciousness permeates the organization's DNA, ensuring that proactive risk management becomes a part of the organization's ethos.

In conclusion, the benefits of risk assessments run the gamut from strategic decision-making and resource optimization to regulatory compliance, stakeholder trust, resilience-building, and seizing opportunities. As a multifaceted practice, risk assessment is not confined to a singular domain; it infuses every aspect of an organization's functioning with greater insight and preparedness. Organizations that embrace risk assessments embark on a journey of empowerment, equipped to navigate the complexities of the business environment with strategic precision and poise. The dividends of this proactive approach are manifold, positioning organizations for sustained success in a landscape where uncertainties are constant companions.

New Developments in Risk Assessment

The landscape of risk assessment is in a perpetual state of evolution, mirroring the dynamic and complex nature of the modern business environment. New developments in risk assessment are continuously shaping the way organizations identify, evaluate, and mitigate risks. From technological advancements to changing regulatory frameworks, these developments are pivotal in ensuring that risk assessment remains a relevant and effective tool for organizations to navigate uncertainties.

Central to these new developments is the integration of data analytics, which has fundamentally transformed the landscape of risk assessment. Organizations now harness the power of data to gain deeper insights into potential risks and their effects. The integration of data analytics enables organizations to conduct predictive risk assessments, empowering them to anticipate potential challenges and take preemptive actions.

The emergence of AI and ML technologies has brought unprecedented precision and automation to risk assessment processes. These technologies are capable of analyzing massive datasets with remarkable speed and accuracy, allowing organizations to identify hidden correlations and potential risks that might have otherwise gone unnoticed. Machine learning algorithms can continuously learn and adapt, refining risk assessment models based on real-time data.

Regulatory frameworks governing industries and sectors are in a constant state of flux, reflecting the evolving global economic and political landscape. The effects of regulatory changes on risk assessment cannot be understated. Organizations must be agile in adapting their risk assessment methodologies to align with new regulations. This necessitates a comprehensive understanding of the regulatory environment and the ability to integrate regulatory requirements into risk assessment frameworks.

The paradigm of risk assessment has expanded beyond traditional financial and operational risks to encompass environmental, social, and governance (ESG) considerations. The global shift toward sustainable practices has elevated ESG factors to the forefront of organizational priorities. As a result, organizations are integrating ESG considerations into their risk assessment processes. This entails evaluating risks related to climate change, social responsibility, diversity and inclusion, and ethical governance.

In an era characterized by digitization and interconnectedness, cybersecurity and digital risks have emerged as omnipresent challenges for organizations. Risk assessment has had to adapt to this new reality by incorporating cybersecurity as a core consideration. This involves assessing the vulnerabilities and potential consequences of cyberattacks, data breaches, and privacy infringements.

Global supply chains are becoming increasingly intricate and interconnected, exposing organizations to a myriad of supply chain risks. These risks can range from disruptions caused by geopolitical events to vulnerabilities in supplier networks. To address this, organizations are adopting a holistic approach to supply chain risk assessment. This comprehensive assessment enables organizations to identify critical nodes, potential vulnerabilities, and alternate sourcing options to mitigate supply chain disruptions.

The realization that human behavior can be a significant source of risk has prompted organizations to integrate behavioral risk assessments into their frameworks. This involves analyzing employee behaviors, decision-making patterns, and adherence to protocols.

Organizations are leveraging psychological insights to identify potential human-related risks that might arise from errors, misconduct, or lack of adherence to procedures.

The traditional approach to risk assessment often revolves around historical data and known risks. However, new developments have introduced the integration of scenario analysis, which involves assessing the potential effects of plausible yet unexpected events. By simulating various scenarios, organizations can develop contingency plans, refine their risk responses, and enhance overall resilience.

Modern risk assessment methodologies are increasingly collaborative in nature, leveraging the collective intelligence of various stakeholders within and outside the organization. Cross-functional teams, comprising individuals with diverse backgrounds and expertise, collaborate to identify, evaluate, and prioritize risks. Collaborative risk assessments enhance the accuracy of risk identification and empower organizations to adopt a comprehensive risk mitigation strategy.

In a world characterized by rapid technological advancements, shifting regulations, and interconnected economies, the landscape of risk assessment is continuously evolving. The integration of data analytics, AI, and ML technologies is revolutionizing risk assessment methodologies, enabling organizations to be proactive and precise in their risk management efforts. As organizations navigate this ever-evolving landscape, their ability to embrace these new developments in risk assessment will determine their resilience, agility, and preparedness in the face of uncertainties.

Chapter 8:
Incident Response Planning

In today's rapidly evolving digital landscape where cyberthreats and security breaches have become more sophisticated and pervasive, the implementation of an incident response plan (IRP) has emerged as a critical necessity for organizations across all sectors. An IRP is a comprehensive strategy that outlines the steps an organization will take in the event of a data breach or any other form of cybersecurity breach. This chapter delves into the significance of having a well-defined incident response plan, emphasizing the crucial role it plays in mitigating the consequences of security incidents, ensuring business continuity, and safeguarding an organization's reputation.

The Cybersecurity Threat Landscape: A Growing Imperative for IRP

The modern threat landscape is characterized by an alarming increase in cyberattacks, ranging from data breaches and ransomware attacks to phishing and insider threats. With cybercriminals employing advanced techniques to breach even the most fortified security infrastructures, organizations are left vulnerable to a variety of risks that can compromise sensitive information, disrupt operations, and lead to financial losses. As a result, a robust and well-structured incident response plan has become paramount to swiftly detect, contain, and recover from security incidents.

The Essence of Incident Response Planning

Incident response planning entails a systematic approach to managing and mitigating security incidents, with the primary goal of minimizing the effects on an organization's operations, reputation, and bottom line. This process involves the collaboration of various stakeholders, including IT teams, legal experts, public relations professionals, and senior management. The incident response plan is a comprehensive document that outlines the roles and responsibilities of each stakeholder, defines the processes for identifying and assessing incidents, and prescribes the steps to be taken during and after an incident.

Mitigating Financial Losses and Operational Disruptions

The financial repercussions of a security incident can be staggering. A robust incident response plan can significantly minimize these losses by facilitating the identification of the breach's source, determining the extent of the damage, and prompting the organization to implement immediate measures to contain the incident. Swift containment reduces the duration of the incident, which mitigates financial losses associated with business disruptions. Moreover, having a well-prepared IRP can expedite recovery efforts, reducing downtime and ensuring that the organization can resume its normal operations as quickly as possible.

Preserving Reputation and Customer Trust

The aftermath of a security incident often extends beyond financial losses and operational disruptions. A breach can severely damage an organization's reputation and erode the trust of customers, partners, and stakeholders. In an era in which data privacy is paramount, customers expect organizations to safeguard their personal and sensitive information. An incident response plan is crucial in restoring trust by demonstrating the organization's commitment to transparency, accountability, and swift action. Effective communication strategies outlined in the IRP ensure that stakeholders are promptly informed about the incident, the measures being taken to address it, and the steps being taken to prevent future breaches.

Legal and Regulatory Compliance

The importance of incident response planning extends beyond financial losses and reputation management. With an increasing number of data protection regulations and privacy laws coming into effect, organizations are legally obligated to protect the personal information of their customers and stakeholders. An incident response plan provides a structured framework for ensuring compliance with these regulations. It outlines the necessary steps to assess the extent of the breach, notify affected parties, and liaise with regulatory authorities in a timely manner. By adhering to these guidelines, organizations can avoid hefty fines and legal liabilities that may arise from noncompliance.

Challenges in Implementing an Effective Incident Response Plan

Although the benefits of an incident response plan are evident, organizations often encounter challenges when it comes to implementation. One of the major challenges is the lack of awareness among employees regarding the plan's existence and their roles in its execution. An IRP can be effective only if all stakeholders are well informed and trained to respond swiftly and effectively to an incident. Additionally, resource constraints, especially in smaller organizations, can hinder the implementation of a comprehensive plan. Crafting an effective IRP requires a significant investment of time, effort, and resources, including the acquisition of cutting-edge cybersecurity tools and technologies.

Best Practices for an Effective Incident Response Plan

To overcome these challenges, organizations can adopt several best practices to ensure the successful implementation of an incident response plan. Regular training and drills can familiarize employees with the plan and their roles in executing it. This not only ensures a faster response but also helps identify any gaps in the plan that need to be addressed. Collaboration and communication are key; involving cross-functional teams and ensuring open lines of communication between departments can facilitate a swift response. Additionally, partnering with external cybersecurity experts can provide organizations with the necessary expertise to develop and refine their IRPs.

The complexities and nuances of incident response planning go beyond the surface benefits, necessitating a deeper understanding of the core elements that contribute to its significance. One of the central aspects is the proactive nature of an incident response plan. Instead of being reactive to a security breach or data compromise, organizations with a well-structured IRP are empowered to take preemptive actions to mitigate risks. This proactive stance ensures that potential threats are identified and addressed before they escalate into full-blown security incidents, guarding the organization from severe damage.

Another key aspect of an incident response plan is its role in fostering a culture of preparedness. By ingraining a sense of readiness and awareness among employees, organizations create an environment in which everyone is vigilant and capable of recognizing early signs of a potential breach. This cultural shift enhances the organization's overall security posture and allows for quicker detection and response to incidents. A culture of preparedness also involves conducting regular training and simulations, thereby ensuring that employees are well equipped to execute the IRP effectively.

The complexity of today's technology landscape has led to an interconnected web of systems, applications, and devices. An incident affecting one part of an organization's infrastructure can quickly propagate to other areas. The interconnectedness of systems therefore necessitates a well-coordinated response across various departments and functions. An incident response plan provides a road map for collaboration, ensuring that all stakeholders know role and responsibilities during a security incident. This collaboration extends to external partners such as cybersecurity firms and legal counsel, who can provide specialized expertise to handle specific aspects of the incident.

Furthermore, the dynamic nature of cyberthreats demands that organizations take an adaptive and iterative approach to incident response planning. Organizations must continually assess and update their IRPs to account for emerging threats, technological advancements, and changes in the organization's infrastructure. Regular reviews ensure that the plan remains relevant and effective in the face of evolving risks. This adaptability is crucial in an environment in which threat actors are constantly devising new strategies to breach an organization's defenses.

Addressing Human Factors in Incident Response

Although technology plays a pivotal role in incident response, the human factor remains equally important. Employees are often the first line of defense against security breaches. However, they can also unwittingly become conduits for cyberattacks through social engineering tactics such as phishing. The success of an incident response plan hinges on educating employees about potential threats, ensuring that they are cautious and well informed in their digital interactions.

Recognizing that employees can be both the greatest asset and the weakest link, organizations need to provide comprehensive cybersecurity training. This includes educating employees about the latest phishing techniques, malware threats, and social engineering strategies. Regular training sessions help employees recognize suspicious activities and take appropriate actions, such as reporting potential incidents promptly.

Real-World Cases Highlighting the Need for Incident Response

Several high-profile cyber incidents underscore the importance of a well-implemented incident response plan. The Equifax breach of 2017, which compromised the personal information of 143 million people, demonstrated the need for swift and effective incident response. Equifax faced widespread criticism for its delayed and inadequate response, which resulted in significant damage to its reputation and substantial legal consequences. This incident serves as a stark reminder of the cascading effects of an inadequate incident response plan.

Similarly, the ransomware attack on the city of Atlanta, Georgia, in 2018 highlighted the effects of an unprepared response to cyberthreats. The attack crippled various city services, leading to financial losses and service disruptions. A lack of comprehensive incident response procedures exacerbated the situation, emphasizing the critical role of an IRP in minimizing the consequences of such attacks.

Mitigating Financial Losses

The financial repercussions of a security incident can be overwhelming, encompassing direct financial losses, regulatory fines, legal fees, and costs associated with reputational damage. An incident response plan aids organizations in mitigating these financial losses by orchestrating a rapid response that curtails the incident's spread and scope. Timely containment and recovery measures, as guided by the IRP, limit the duration of the incident, translating to reduced financial damages and operational disruptions.

Protecting Brand Reputation

In an era defined by digital interconnectedness, a brand's reputation is a fragile yet invaluable asset. A security incident, if mishandled, can have enduring and far-reaching consequences for an organization's reputation. Customers, partners, and stakeholders expect organizations to safeguard their data and privacy. An incident response plan is crucial in managing the communication and public relations aspects of an incident. By having a well-structured plan in place, organizations can navigate the delicate process of informing stakeholders, addressing concerns, and demonstrating a commitment to transparency and accountability.

Ensuring Legal and Regulatory Compliance

The regulatory landscape governing data protection and cybersecurity is rapidly evolving, with stringent regulations mandating that organizations safeguard sensitive information. The European Union's GDPR, the CCPA, and various industry-specific regulations underscore the need for organizations to have effective incident response plans. An IRP ensures that organizations adhere to the legal obligations of reporting incidents, notifying affected parties, and liaising with regulatory authorities within stipulated timelines. By embedding these compliance requirements within the plan, organizations avoid legal liabilities and reputational damage stemming from noncompliance.

Challenges in Incident Response Planning

Despite the evident benefits, implementing a robust incident response plan can be fraught with challenges. One of the key challenges is the complexity of modern infrastructures, characterized by cloud environments, remote-work arrangements, and third-party integrations. Ensuring seamless coordination and communication among diverse systems and stakeholders is imperative for an effective IRP. Additionally, organizations often struggle with resource constraints, in terms of both budget and expertise. Crafting an incident response plan necessitates investment in training, technologies, and cybersecurity personnel who are well versed in the intricacies of incident response.

The Future of Incident Response: Anticipating Developments

As the threat landscape continues to evolve, the future of incident response planning will likely be characterized by even greater automation and integration of artificial intelligence. AI-driven tools can rapidly analyze vast amounts of data to identify anomalies, enabling organizations to detect and respond to incidents in real time. Moreover, advancements in threat intelligence and predictive analytics will provide organizations with the ability to foresee potential threats and take proactive measures.

Furthermore, the ongoing evolution of regulatory frameworks, such as the GDPR and the CCPA, will drive organizations to develop more sophisticated and tailored incident response plans to ensure compliance. Organizations will need to navigate the intricacies of reporting timelines, data breach notifications, and other legal requirements, which an effective incident response plan can facilitate.

In conclusion, the implementation of an incident response plan is no longer a mere precaution but a critical necessity in today's digital landscape. The potential financial losses, operational disruptions, reputation damage, and legal liabilities associated with security incidents underscore the need for organizations to have a comprehensive and well-structured IRP in place. An effective incident response plan not only minimizes the consequences of security breaches but also fosters trust among stakeholders and ensures compliance with evolving data protection regulations. As organizations continue to navigate the evolving threat landscape, the presence of a robust incident response plan is a strategic imperative that can determine an organization's resilience and long-term success.

Chapter 9:
Identity and Access Management

Identity and access management (IAM) has become a critical component of modern organizations' cybersecurity strategies. In today's digital landscape, where cyberthreats and data breaches are on the rise, effective IAM practices are essential for protecting sensitive information, ensuring regulatory compliance, and mitigating security risks. IAM refers to the processes, technologies, and policies that enable organizations to manage and control user identities, access privileges, and authentication mechanisms. It encompasses a range of activities, including user provisioning, authentication, authorization, and identity lifecycle management. The importance of IAM cannot be overstated, as it forms the foundation for secure and controlled access to critical resources, systems, and data.

One of the primary reasons IAM is crucial for organizations is the need to protect sensitive data. With the increasing reliance on digital systems and the proliferation of cloud services, organizations collect and store vast amounts of sensitive information, including customer data, intellectual property, and financial records. Without proper IAM practices in place, unauthorized individuals can gain access to this data, resulting in data breaches, financial losses, reputational damage, and legal consequences. Effective IAM ensures that only authorized individuals can access sensitive data, reducing the risk of data breaches and safeguarding the organization's valuable assets.

IAM also plays a vital role in ensuring regulatory compliance. Many industries, such as health care, finance, and government, are subject to strict regulations regarding the protection of sensitive information. Compliance with regulations such HIPAA, PCI DSS, and the GDPR requires organizations to implement robust IAM practices. IAM helps organizations meet compliance requirements by enforcing access controls, maintaining audit logs, and demonstrating accountability for data access and usage. Noncompliance with these regulations can lead to severe penalties, fines, and damage to an organization's reputation. Furthermore, IAM enhances overall security posture by reducing the risk of insider threats and unauthorized access. Insider threats, whether intentional or accidental, pose a significant risk to organizations' security. IAM solutions help prevent unauthorized access by implementing strong authentication mechanisms, role-based access controls, and user-provisioning processes. By ensuring that individuals have the appropriate level of access privileges based on their roles and responsibilities, IAM minimizes the risk of insider misuse and unauthorized actions.

IAM also simplifies the management of user identities and access privileges across complex IT environments. In large organizations with multiple systems, applications, and user accounts, manually managing user access can be time consuming, error prone, and inefficient. IAM solutions streamline user provisioning and deprovisioning processes, enabling organizations to automate user lifecycle management. This automation not only saves time and resources but also reduces the likelihood of human errors, such as granting excessive privileges or failing to revoke access when needed. Moreover, IAM promotes user productivity and convenience by providing seamless and secure access to resources. With the increasing adoption of cloud services and mobile devices, users need to access organizational resources from anywhere, at any time, and from any device. IAM technologies facilitate secure single sign-on capabilities, enabling users to access multiple systems and applications using a single set of credentials. This eliminates the need for users to remember multiple passwords, improving user experience and productivity while maintaining strong security measures.

One of the primary reasons IAM is important for an enterprise is the need to protect sensitive data and ensure data privacy. Enterprises handle vast amounts of valuable and confidential information, including customer data, financial records, and intellectual property. Unauthorized access to this information can result in financial loss, reputational damage, legal implications, and compliance violations. IAM provides mechanisms for verifying and authenticating users, ensuring that only authorized individuals have access to specific resources.

By implementing IAM controls, enterprises can enforce least-privilege principles, granting users the appropriate level of access based on their roles and responsibilities. This helps minimize the risk of data breaches and unauthorized data access.

IAM also enhances security by enabling effective identity management and user provisioning. With the proliferation of cloud-based services, mobile devices, and remote working, enterprises face the challenge of managing a diverse and dynamic user population. IAM solutions offer centralized user-management capabilities, allowing organizations to streamline the process of creating, modifying, and disabling user accounts. By implementing IAM, enterprises can enforce strong password policies, enforce multifactor authentication, and promptly revoke access for users who no longer require it. These measures reduce the risk of compromised user credentials and unauthorized access to systems and applications.

Moreover, IAM facilitates compliance with regulatory requirements and industry standards. Many sectors, such as finance, health care, and government, are subject to strict data protection regulations. IAM frameworks assist organizations in meeting these compliance obligations by providing audit trails, access controls, and user-activity monitoring. IAM also supports the principle of segregation of duties, ensuring that critical operations are performed by multiple individuals to prevent fraudulent activities. Compliance with regulations such as the GDPR, HIPAA, and PCI DSS can be achieved through the implementation of robust IAM practices.

Efficiency and productivity are additional advantages of IAM for enterprises. IAM solutions offer self-service capabilities, allowing users to manage their own access rights and reset passwords, reducing the burden on IT support teams. This self-service functionality empowers users, enhances user experience, and improves overall productivity. Additionally, IAM systems enable single sign-on capabilities, allowing users to authenticate once and gain access to multiple systems and applications. This eliminates the need to remember multiple usernames and passwords, simplifying the user experience and reducing the risk of weak or reused passwords.

IAM also aids in managing third-party access and external users. Enterprises often collaborate with external partners, contractors, and vendors who require access to specific systems and data. IAM solutions provide mechanisms to extend access privileges to these external entities while maintaining control and visibility of their activities. By implementing IAM, enterprises can enforce policies and permissions for external users, ensuring that their access is limited to the necessary resources and time frames.

Identity and access management (IAM) is a critical component of modern cybersecurity practices, and many corporations have adopted IAM solutions to enhance their security posture and streamline access to resources. One notable example is Microsoft, which leverages IAM extensively in its Azure Active Directory (Azure AD) service. Azure AD allows organizations to manage user identities, enforce multifactor authentication, control access to resources, and integrate with various applications. With Azure AD, Microsoft provides a secure and seamless authentication experience across its cloud-based services, such as Microsoft 365 and Azure, benefiting millions of organizations worldwide.

Another corporation that heavily relies on IAM is Airbnb. As a leading online marketplace for short-term rentals, Airbnb places great emphasis on user identity and security. IAM plays a crucial role in Airbnb's platform by ensuring the verification of hosts and guests. Through various IAM measures, including user authentication, verification processes, and reputation systems, Airbnb builds trust and maintains a secure environment for its users. IAM helps protect users' personal information and ensures that only legitimate and verified individuals can participate in the Airbnb community.

Amazon, a global e-commerce and cloud computing company, also uses IAM extensively to manage user access to its wide range of services. Through AWS IAM, businesses can control and secure access to their AWS resources, such as compute power, storage, and databases. IAM enables organizations to create and manage user identities, assign granular access permissions, enforce multifactor authentication, and integrate with existing directory services. This allows businesses to maintain tight control over their cloud infrastructure and data, ensuring that only authorized personnel can access critical resources.

In the financial sector, JPMorgan Chase relies on IAM solutions to protect its systems and sensitive financial data. IAM plays a pivotal role in providing secure access to JPMorgan Chase's resources and ensuring compliance with industry regulations. The company employs IAM technologies for user authentication, access controls, and identity governance. These measures help prevent unauthorized access, strengthen data protection, and ensure that customer information remains confidential. IAM is a fundamental part of JPMorgan Chase's security infrastructure, enabling the organization to maintain trust and security for its customers and stakeholders.

This example demonstrates how corporations can leverage IAM to enhance security, streamline access management, and protect sensitive data. IAM solutions play a vital role in ensuring that only authorized individuals have access to resources, guarding against data breaches, and maintaining compliance with regulatory requirements. As businesses continue to embrace digital transformation, the adoption of IAM becomes increasingly crucial in establishing robust security practices and protecting valuable assets.

IAM also supports the principle of least privilege, which restricts user access rights to only the necessary resources and privileges required to perform their job functions. By implementing the principle of least privilege, organizations can minimize the potential consequences of compromised user accounts or insider threats. IAM solutions enable organizations to enforce granular access controls, ensuring that users have the appropriate level of access rights based on their roles and responsibilities. This reduces the attack surface and limits the potential damage that can be caused by malicious actors.

IAM is a critical component of organizations' cybersecurity strategies. It provides the foundation for secure access to critical resources, protects sensitive information, ensures regulatory compliance, mitigates security risks, and enhances overall security posture. With the increasing frequency and sophistication of cyberthreats, implementing robust IAM practices has become imperative for organizations of all sizes and industries. By adopting effective IAM solutions, organizations can establish strong access controls, enforce least privilege, automate user provisioning, and enhance user productivity while maintaining a secure environment. IAM is not just a technology but a comprehensive approach that aligns people, processes, and technologies to protect valuable assets and enable secure and controlled access in today's digital world.

Challenges of Implementing IAM

Despite the many advantages of IAM, implementing IAM in an enterprise comes with its own set of challenges. One of the primary challenges is balancing security and usability. IAM controls, such as complex passwords and multifactor authentication, can sometimes inconvenience users and affect productivity. Striking the right balance between security and user experience requires careful consideration and user feedback to ensure that IAM measures do not hinder legitimate user activities. Another challenge is the complexity of IAM integration with diverse systems and applications. Enterprises often have a heterogeneous IT environment with various legacy systems, cloud services, and on-premises applications.

With careful planning and effective strategies, these challenges can be overcome. One approach is to develop a comprehensive IAM strategy that aligns with the business objectives and requirements of the enterprise. This strategy should include clear goals, a road map, and a prioritized approach to implementation. By defining a well-thought-out strategy, enterprises can ensure that IAM initiatives are properly scoped, resources are allocated appropriately, and potential roadblocks are anticipated and addressed.

Another key aspect is to establish strong leadership and governance for IAM implementation. This involves having executive sponsorship and dedicated IAM teams and fostering cross-functional collaboration. Effective governance helps in making informed decisions, resolving conflicts, and maintaining alignment between IAM and business objectives. Engaging stakeholders throughout the IAM implementation process is also crucial. This includes involving business units, IT teams, security teams, and end users in the planning, design, and testing phases. Engaging stakeholders helps in gathering valuable insights, addressing concerns, and ensuring that IAM solutions meet the needs of the organization. Clear and frequent communication is vital to keeping all stakeholders informed about the progress, benefits, and challenges of IAM implementation. Conducting a thorough risk assessment and prioritization is another important step in overcoming challenges. Enterprises should analyze existing vulnerabilities and identify the most critical areas for IAM implementation. By focusing on high-risk areas first, enterprises can mitigate potential security risks and allocate resources more effectively.

Choosing the right IAM solution is also crucial for successful implementation. Enterprises should carefully evaluate different IAM vendors and solutions to ensure they meet their specific requirements. The selected solution should align with the enterprise's technology infrastructure, scalability needs, and future growth plans. It is important to consider factors such as ease of integration, user experience, and the ability to support diverse authentication methods. Building a strong IAM team with the necessary skills and expertise is also vital. An enterprise should invest in training and development programs to ensure that its IAM team is equipped with the knowledge and capabilities to implement and manage IAM effectively. This includes staying updated with the latest industry trends and best practices. Furthermore, enterprises should leverage industry standards and frameworks for IAM implementation. Compliance with internationally accepted standards such as ISO 27001, NIST, and GDPR can provide a solid foundation for implementing IAM practices that align with regulatory requirements. These standards offer guidance on various aspects of IAM, including access control, identity lifecycle management, and authentication mechanisms. Regular monitoring, evaluation, and adjustment of IAM processes and controls are essential for ongoing success. Enterprises should establish a way to collect user feedback, identify areas for improvement, and make necessary adjustments to the IAM implementation. This iterative approach ensures that IAM practices evolve and adapt to changing business needs and emerging security threats. IAM is a critical component for enterprises operating in the digital era. It offers a comprehensive framework that enables organizations to effectively manage user identities, control access to resources, and ensure the security of sensitive data. The importance of IAM cannot be overstated, as it provides numerous benefits such as enhanced security measures, data privacy, regulatory compliance, operational efficiency, and streamlined user management. Implementing IAM requires careful planning, a well-defined strategy, and a focus on usability. It is essential for enterprises to consider the unique needs and requirements of their organization, ensuring that the IAM solution aligns seamlessly with existing systems and workflows.

By investing in IAM, enterprises can establish a robust security posture that mitigates the risks associated with unauthorized access, data breaches, and insider threats. Furthermore, IAM plays a vital role in maintaining trust with customers, partners, and stakeholders. In an interconnected world where data breaches and cyber-attacks are prevalent, organizations that prioritize IAM demonstrate their commitment to safeguarding sensitive information and protecting valuable assets. By effectively managing identities, controlling access, and implementing strong authentication mechanisms, enterprises can build a reputation for being trustworthy and reliable.

IAM is an indispensable tool for enterprises looking to strengthen their security infrastructure and navigate the complexities of the digital landscape. By embracing IAM solutions and best practices, organizations can proactively address security risks, improve operational efficiency, and foster a culture of trust and confidence in their digital interactions. As technology continues to advance, IAM will remain a critical element in safeguarding identities and ensuring secure access to resources.

Chapter 10 :
Third-Party Vendor Risk Management

In the interconnected landscape of modern business, third-party relationships have become integral to the functioning of organizations. These external entities, including suppliers, vendors, and service providers, contribute significantly to delivering goods, services, and support. However, these collaborations also introduce inherent risks that can challenge an organization's security, reputation, and overall operations.

The significance of third-party risk management lies in its ability to ensure that business partners and vendors operate within a secure framework. This approach balances the benefits of collaboration with the need to safeguard assets and integrity. Outsourcing functions to third parties offers cost savings, expertise, and flexibility, but it also introduces vulnerabilities that can disrupt operations and compromise data.

Managing third-party risks is complex because of the diverse nature of these relationships and the dynamic business environment. Each third party operates with unique protocols and security standards, requiring tailored risk assessments. The growing reliance on digital platforms and technologies introduces new avenues for cyberthreats, necessitating assessments of the digital ecosystem alongside the physical supply chain.

Navigating these risks demands robust strategies. Thorough risk assessments evaluating vulnerabilities in a business's external relationships are crucial. Factors such as data sensitivity, access privileges, and third-party cybersecurity protocols must be considered. Clear contractual agreements outlining security expectations, data protection measures, and incident-reporting procedures are essential. Continuous monitoring of third-party activities helps identify anomalies that may indicate potential risks.

As the digital landscape evolves, so do third-party risks. The rise of cloud-based solutions, IoT devices, and application programming interfaces (APIs) brings new vulnerabilities. Third-party risk management strategies must adapt to address these emerging threats. Regulatory frameworks such as GDPR and CCPA heighten legal obligations concerning third-party data security and privacy. Balancing compliance with maintaining efficient third-party relationships is essential.

Real-world instances emphasize the consequences of neglecting third-party risk management. The 2013 Target breach, exploiting a vulnerability in a third-party HVAC vendor's system, led to data theft and reputational damage. The 2017 Equifax breach, attributed to a third-party software vulnerability, exposed sensitive data of millions. These cases highlight how one compromised third party can affect an organization's security, financial stability, and public image.

In the ever-evolving realm of modern business, the relationships that organizations establish with third parties have transcended mere transactional interactions to become pivotal components of their overall operations. However, these collaborations are not without their share of intricacies and inherent risks that have the potential to test an organization's resilience, tarnish its reputation, and even compromise its very existence.

At the heart of the matter lies the overarching significance of third-party risk management—a discipline that has evolved to counterbalance the intricate dynamics of external relationships with the imperative of maintaining robust security frameworks. This proactive approach creates a harmonious equilibrium, allowing organizations to leverage the myriad benefits of collaboration while safeguarding their assets, data, and the trust of their stakeholders.

The practice of outsourcing various business functions to third parties offers undeniable advantages, including cost efficiencies, specialized expertise, and heightened operational flexibility. Yet the very act of extending business operations beyond the confines of the organization's walls introduces inherent vulnerabilities. These vulnerabilities can potentially disrupt regular operations, compromise sensitive data, and expose the organization to regulatory penalties. Thus, the strategic importance of third-party risk management becomes evident, as it seeks to strike a delicate equilibrium between embracing external partnerships and mitigating the associated risks.

However, embarking on this endeavor is not without its challenges, and navigating the complexities of third-party risk management necessitates a meticulous understanding of its various dimensions. One of the primary challenges lies in the sheer diversity of third parties themselves. Moreover, the relentless advance of digitalization and the increasing reliance on interconnected technologies further exacerbate the intricacies of third-party risk management. The very attributes that drive efficiency and innovation—cloud-based solutions, internet of things (IoT) devices, and application programming interfaces (APIs)—also open up new avenues for vulnerabilities. This dynamic calls for a reimagining of risk assessment strategies that extends beyond the physical supply chain to encompass the digital ecosystem of third parties.

To surmount these challenges, organizations must embrace a set of best practices that underpin effective third-party risk management. Foremost among these practices is the need for a comprehensive risk assessment process. This process delves into the vulnerabilities inherent in each external relationship, taking into account factors such as the sensitivity of the data being shared, access privileges, and the cybersecurity protocols of the third party. Such assessments lay the foundation for informed decision-making and risk mitigation strategies.

Equally paramount is the establishment of clear and robust contractual agreements with third parties. These agreements need to delineate security expectations, data protection measures, and incident-reporting procedures. Such contractual clarity not only establishes a common understanding but also sets the stage for a shared commitment to upholding security standards.

Continual monitoring of third-party activities is another vital pillar of effective third-party risk management. The digital landscape is dynamic, and external entities' risk postures can shift rapidly. Organizations need to proactively identify any deviations or anomalies in the behavior of their third-party partners, as these could indicate potential risks. This necessitates the integration of risk monitoring into the organization's broader risk management framework.

As the digital landscape continues to evolve, the terrain of third-party risk management is also subject to transformation. Regulatory frameworks such as the European Union's GDPR and the CCPA have heightened the legal obligations of organizations concerning the security and privacy of third-party data. Organizations must adapt to these regulations while maintaining efficient and productive relationships with their external partners.

Real-world instances stand as stark reminders of the consequences of neglecting third-party risk management. The notorious 2013 breach at Target Corporation serves as a telling case. Cybercriminals exploited a vulnerability in a third-party HVAC vendor's system, infiltrating Target's network and leading to data theft on a massive scale. This breach not only resulted in financial losses but also had a far-reaching effect on the company's reputation and eroded customer trust.

The 2017 Equifax breach further underscores the cascading repercussions of inadequate third-party risk management. A vulnerability in a third-party software allowed cybercriminals to access sensitive financial data of nearly 143 million consumers, a massive breach that led to substantial financial and reputational damage. These real-world cases exemplify how the seemingly innocuous vulnerabilities arising from external partnerships can escalate into full-scale security breaches with far-reaching consequences. The incidents serve as a stark reminder of the necessity for robust third-party risk management strategies that account for the intricate nuances of external relationships.

Neglecting third-party risk management is akin to leaving a potential time bomb unchecked. Financial losses, reputational damage, legal consequences, and eroded stakeholder trust are among the grim outcomes that can materialize. In a world where collaboration and interconnectedness drive growth and innovation, comprehensive third-party risk management strategies stand as a pivotal pillar for safeguarding sustainable growth and security. As organizations continue to forge external partnerships, embracing the tenets of third-party risk management is an imperative that resonates not only in boardrooms but also across every facet of the modern business ecosystem.

In other words, third-party risk management is a vital discipline in a collaborative business landscape. External relationships introduce multifaceted challenges that demand a comprehensive approach to risk mitigation. Adhering to best practices, conducting thorough risk assessments, and adapting to the evolving digital landscape are essential. Neglecting third-party risk management can result in financial losses, reputational damage, and legal consequences. As organizations continue to partner, comprehensive third-party risk management strategies remain crucial for sustainable growth and security.

The importance of third-party vendor risk management in today's business landscape cannot be overstated. This risk management serves as a vigilant guardian, ensuring that the extended network of business partners and vendors operates within a framework of controlled risk. This proactive stance enables organizations to harness the benefits of collaboration while concurrently safeguarding their critical assets, sensitive information, and the trust of their stakeholders.

Third-party vendor risk management offers a structured approach to the complexities introduced by external partnerships. The essence of its significance lies in its ability to strike a delicate equilibrium between reaping the rewards of collaboration and mitigating the potential pitfalls. As organizations continue to outsource various functions and processes, including those involving critical data and sensitive operations, the need for a robust risk management strategy becomes all the more evident.

Yet effective third-party vendor risk management isn't without its share of challenges. Each third party operates within unique operational protocols and security standards, necessitating a tailored risk assessment approach for each. This diversity further underscores the necessity of a comprehensive strategy that covers a wide spectrum of potential risks, including cybersecurity vulnerabilities and data privacy concerns.

The digital transformation sweeping across industries introduces both opportunities and vulnerabilities in the realm of third-party partnerships. The rise of cloud-based solutions, the proliferation of IoT devices, and the expanding use of APIs provide new avenues for risks to infiltrate organizations through external channels. This dynamic underscores the importance of an adaptable and agile third-party vendor risk management strategy that can identify and mitigate these emerging threats.

Chapter 11:
Security Awareness Training

In today's digital landscape, where cyberthreats are constantly evolving, organizations must prioritize security awareness training as a crucial component of their overall security strategy. Security awareness training helps employees understand the risks, recognize potential threats, and adopt best practices to protect sensitive information and the organization's assets. This chapter explores the significance of security awareness training, its key elements, and effective strategies for building a security-aware culture within an organization.

The Importance of Security Awareness Training

In today's interconnected and digital world, organizations face an ever-growing number of cybersecurity threats. Malicious actors are constantly devising new methods to exploit vulnerabilities and gain unauthorized access to sensitive information. Cyberthreats continue to evolve and become more sophisticated. From phishing attacks and social engineering to malware and ransomware, organizations face a wide range of potential risks. However, many of these threats can be mitigated through employee education and awareness. Security awareness training helps employees recognize common attack vectors, understand the importance of safeguarding sensitive data, and develop good security hygiene practices.

Benefits of Security Awareness Training

The major advantages of providing regular security awareness training for all employees in an organization are as follows:

- **Risk Mitigation:** One of the primary benefits of security awareness training is the mitigation of potential risks. By educating employees about the types of threats they may encounter, organizations can significantly reduce the likelihood of successful attacks. Employees who are aware of common tactics such as phishing emails and malicious attachments are less likely to fall victim to these scams.

- **Enhanced Security Culture:** Security awareness training helps foster a culture of security within an organization. When employees are educated about cybersecurity best practices, they become active participants in safeguarding the organization's assets. This culture of security extends beyond the training sessions and becomes ingrained in daily work practices, leading to a more resilient and security-conscious workforce.

- **Protection of Sensitive Data:** Data breaches can have severe consequences for organizations, including financial loss, reputational damage, and legal repercussions. Security awareness training emphasizes the importance of protecting sensitive data, both at rest and in transit. Employees learn how to handle data securely, identify potential vulnerabilities, and implement appropriate security measures.

- **Compliance and Regulatory Requirements:** Many industries are subject to strict compliance and regulatory standards, such as the GDPR and HIPAA. Security awareness training helps organizations meet these requirements by ensuring that employees understand their responsibilities and obligations regarding data protection and privacy.

Security awareness training plays a crucial role in mitigating the risks associated with cybersecurity and protecting organizations from potential threats. In today's digital landscape, where cyberattacks are becoming increasingly sophisticated, organizations must recognize that employees can be the weakest link in the security chain. Employees, whether intentionally or unintentionally, can expose sensitive information or fall victim to social engineering tactics. This makes it essential for organizations to invest in comprehensive security awareness programs to educate and empower their workforce.

Numerous cases serve as reminders of the critical role employees play in cybersecurity. One notable case, the "WannaCry" ransomware attack in 2017 affected organizations in over 150 countries. The ransomware exploited a vulnerability in the Windows operating system, encrypting files on infected computers and demanding ransom payments in Bitcoin to restore access. The attack had significant global effects in terms of financial losses and disruptions to resources. It is estimated that the total cost of the attack, including damages and recovery expenses stemming from ransom payments, lost productivity, and cybersecurity investments, was in the hundreds of millions of dollars. In addition to financial losses, the WannaCry attack had a significant effect on the availability of resources. Critical systems in various sectors, including health care, finance, and manufacturing, were disrupted. Some organizations experienced downtime, leading to operational challenges and delayed services. The widespread nature of the attack highlighted the importance of cybersecurity measures and the potential consequences of failing to address vulnerabilities in computer systems.

  The history of security breaches reveals a consistent pattern of human error as a contributing factor. From phishing attacks to social engineering scams, employees are often targeted as an entry point into an organization's network. Cybercriminals exploit human vulnerabilities such as lack of awareness or negligence to gain unauthorized access or steal sensitive information. This highlights the critical role of security awareness training in equipping employees with the knowledge and skills to identify and mitigate these risks. Approaches to effective security awareness training involve a combination of educational initiatives, policies, and ongoing reinforcement. Training programs should cover a wide range of topics, including password hygiene, recognizing phishing attempts, safe browsing practices, data protection, and incident-reporting procedures. Password hygiene is the set of practices individuals use to maintain the security of their passwords and minimize the chances of unauthorized access. It includes creating strong passwords, keeping them private, and regularly changing them. Following good password hygiene is essential for safeguarding personal information and preventing unauthorized individuals from getting into sensitive accounts and data.

Interactive and engaging training materials, such as simulated phishing campaigns and real-world scenarios, can help employees understand the potential consequences of their actions and make more informed decisions.

One company that recognizes the importance of security awareness training is Google. Through its "Phishing Quiz," Google educates users on how to identify and avoid falling victim to phishing attacks. The interactive quiz tests users' knowledge and provides instant feedback, reinforcing the learning process. This approach not only enhances employees' security awareness but also empowers them to take an active role in protecting themselves and the organization. Another example is Cisco, which developed a comprehensive security awareness program called "Securing Our People." The program combines interactive online modules, gamification elements, and ongoing communication to educate employees about various cybersecurity threats and best practices. Cisco's program aims to create a security-conscious culture in which employees are equipped to identify and report potential security incidents promptly.

Effective security awareness training should also address emerging trends and evolving threats. With the increasing prevalence of remote work and the use of personal devices, employees must understand the risks associated with accessing corporate networks from outside the traditional office environment. Training programs should emphasize the importance of secure Wi-Fi connections, the use of virtual private networks, and the protection of sensitive information on personal devices.

Implementing Effective Security Awareness Training

To maximize the effectiveness of security awareness training, organizations should consider the following strategies:

- Tailored Content: Training programs should be customized to address the specific needs and risks of the organization. By focusing on industry-specific threats and incorporating real-world examples, employees can better relate to the training material and understand its relevance to their work environment.

- An Interactive and Engaging Approach: Security awareness training should be engaging and interactive to capture employees' attention and promote active learning. Multimedia elements, gamification, and scenario-based simulations can make the training sessions more enjoyable and effective.

- Ongoing Training and Reinforcement: Security awareness is not a onetime event but a continuous process. Regularly scheduled training sessions, supplemented by newsletters, reminders, and online resources, ensure that employees stay up to date with emerging threats and best practices. Periodic refresher courses and assessments help reinforce key concepts.

- Metrics and Evaluation: It is essential to measure the effectiveness of security awareness training programs. Metrics such as click-through rates on simulated phishing emails, incident-reporting rates, and employee feedback surveys can provide valuable insights into the program's effectiveness and identify areas for improvement.

Security awareness training is a critical component of any comprehensive cybersecurity strategy. By educating employees about the evolving threat landscape and providing them with the necessary knowledge and skills, organizations can significantly reduce the risk of successful attacks and protect sensitive data. A culture of security awareness fosters an environment in which employees are proactive in identifying and mitigating potential risks, enhancing the overall security posture of the corporation. Organizations can also leverage technology to enhance security awareness training. Interactive e-learning platforms, gamification elements, and simulated phishing campaigns can provide hands-on experience and increase employee engagement. Regular assessments and quizzes can measure employees' understanding of security concepts and identify areas that require additional training.

A case in point is Microsoft's Security Awareness Training program. Microsoft offers a comprehensive set of resources and training modules to educate its employees about various security threats and best practices. The program includes simulated phishing campaigns to test employees' susceptibility to phishing attacks and provide targeted training based on the results. By continually assessing employees' knowledge and addressing their areas of weakness, Microsoft ensures that their workforce remains vigilant and is well prepared for evolving cyberthreats.

In addition to addressing technical aspects, security awareness training should emphasize the importance of creating a security-conscious culture within the organization. This involves fostering an environment in which security is viewed as everyone's responsibility and not just the responsibility of the IT department. Encouraging open communication, promoting a reporting culture, and recognizing and rewarding security-conscious behaviors can contribute to building a robust security culture. A notable example is IBM's security awareness program. IBM focuses on creating a culture of security through their "Securing the Human" initiative. The program provides employees with a range of resources, including training modules, videos, newsletters, and posters, to promote awareness and good security practices. By fostering a culture in which security is ingrained in employees' daily activities, IBM strengthens its overall security posture.

Continuous improvement is key to an effective security awareness program. Regular evaluations and feedback from employees can help identify areas for improvement and ensure that the training content remains relevant and engaging. Organizations should also stay abreast of emerging threats and incorporate them into their training materials to address the ever-changing threat landscape.

Key Elements of Security Awareness Training

Security awareness training is a fundamental aspect of building a strong cybersecurity culture within an organization. It equips employees with the knowledge and skills necessary to identify and respond to potential security threats effectively. In this section, we will explore the key elements of an effective security awareness training program, including content development, delivery methods, engagement techniques, and ongoing reinforcement.

Content Development: The first step in designing a successful security awareness training program is developing relevant and engaging content. The content should cover a wide range of security topics, including phishing awareness, password hygiene, social engineering, data protection, and secure remote-work practices. Real-world examples and case studies should be incorporated to demonstrate the potential consequences of security breaches. It is essential to tailor the content to the organization's specific industry, compliance requirements, and security policies to ensure maximum relevance and effectiveness.

Delivery Methods: Choosing the right delivery methods for security awareness training is crucial to engage employees and promote active learning. Traditional classroom-style training may be suitable for certain topics, but organizations should also leverage technology to deliver training in more flexible and interactive ways. Online training modules, webinars, interactive videos, and e-learning platforms allow employees to access the training at their convenience, increasing participation rates and knowledge retention. Mobile-friendly training options are particularly valuable for remote workers or employees on the go.

Engagement Techniques: To capture employees' attention and enhance learning outcomes, employing various engagement techniques is essential. Gamification elements such as quizzes, puzzles, and rewards can make the training experience enjoyable and encourage healthy competition among employees. Scenario-based simulations allow employees to practice their decision-making skills in realistic cybersecurity scenarios. Interactive elements such as click-through exercises or phishing simulations provide hands-on experience in identifying and responding to potential threats.

Ongoing Reinforcement: Effective security awareness training goes beyond a one-time event. It requires ongoing reinforcement to ensure long-term behavior change and knowledge retention. Regularly scheduled refresher courses, newsletters, and security awareness campaigns keep the training content fresh in employees' minds. Security reminders, posters, and screensavers can serve as visual cues to reinforce key security messages throughout the workplace. Providing access to a centralized repository of resources, such as articles, videos, and best practice guidelines, enables employees to refresh their knowledge and stay updated on emerging threats.

Measurement and Evaluation: Measuring the effectiveness of security awareness training is vital to assess it and make informed improvements. Metrics and evaluation methods should be established to track key performance indicators such as the rate of security incidents before and after training, employee participation rates, and knowledge assessment scores. Feedback surveys or focus groups can gather qualitative data on employees' perception of the training program and identify areas for improvement. These metrics and evaluations provide valuable insights into the program's effectiveness and help tailor future training initiatives.

Integration with Organizational Culture

For security awareness training to be truly effective, it must be integrated into the organization's culture and supported by top-level management. Leadership should actively promote the importance of security awareness and lead by example. Incorporating security awareness into performance evaluations and recognition programs reinforces its significance. Integrating security awareness into other organizational processes such as onboarding programs, policy development, and incident response protocols ensures a holistic approach to cybersecurity.

One notable example is the 2013 Target data breach, where cybercriminals gained access to the retailer's network through a third-party vendor. The initial breach occurred when an employee at the vendor fell victim to a phishing attack, inadvertently providing the attackers with credentials to access Target's system. This incident resulted in the theft of personal information from millions of Target customers and had severe financial and reputational consequences for the company. Similarly, in 2014, JPMorgan Chase experienced a significant security breach. The breach was attributed to an employee who fell victim to a spear-phishing attack, compromising log-in credentials. The attackers then gained access to the bank's network, compromising sensitive customer data and affecting the trust of their clients.

These cases illustrate the critical role that employees play in maintaining the security of an organization's data and systems. Despite having robust technical security measures in place, an organization can suffer devastating consequences because of a single employee's mistake or lack of security awareness. Therefore, organizations must prioritize security awareness training to equip their employees with the knowledge and skills necessary to mitigate potential risks.

To ensure the effectiveness of security awareness training, organizations can adopt various approaches. First, training programs should be tailored to the specific needs and roles of employees. Different departments may have varying security requirements, and customizing the training content can make it more relevant and engaging. Furthermore, interactive and engaging training methods can enhance the learning experience. This may include using real-life scenarios, case studies, and interactive simulations to illustrate potential threats and demonstrate proper security practices. When training is interactive and relatable, employees are more likely to understand and internalize the importance of their roles in safeguarding the organization's assets. Regular reinforcement and ongoing education are crucial aspects of effective security awareness training. Security practices and threat landscapes evolve over time, and it is essential to keep employees updated on the latest trends and vulnerabilities. This can be achieved through periodic refresher courses, newsletters, security bulletins, or internal communication channels that highlight recent threats, provide tips, and share best practices.

Collaboration and open communication play vital roles in building a security-conscious workforce. Employees should feel comfortable reporting potential security incidents such as suspicious emails or unauthorized access attempts. Establishing clear reporting procedures and offering guidance on incident reporting can contribute to early detection and mitigation of potential threats. Furthermore, recognizing and rewarding employees who demonstrate good security practices can incentivize others to prioritize security. This can be achieved through acknowledgment programs, incentives, or even including security awareness metrics as part of employees' performance evaluations.

Security awareness training is a vital component of building a strong security culture within an organization. By developing relevant content, using various delivery methods, employing engagement techniques, providing ongoing reinforcement, measuring effectiveness, and integrating training with organizational culture, companies can empower their employees to become the first line of defense against potential security threats. A comprehensive security awareness training program enhances the overall security posture of the organization and fosters a culture of cybersecurity awareness and responsibility.

The importance of security awareness training cannot be overstated in today's digital landscape. Employees are often targeted by cybercriminals as the weakest link in an organization's security chain. By providing comprehensive training, organizations can help their employees recognize and respond to potential threats, reducing the risk of security breaches caused by human error. Real-world cases such as those mentioned earlier serve as reminders of the consequences of inadequate security awareness. Through a combination of educational initiatives, ongoing reinforcement, and a strong security culture, organizations can create a workforce that is proactive, knowledgeable, and capable of defending against cyberthreats.

In conclusion, security awareness training is a crucial component of a comprehensive cybersecurity strategy. Employees are often the first line of defense against cyberthreats, and their knowledge and actions can significantly affect an organization's security posture. By investing in robust and tailored security awareness training programs, organizations can mitigate the risk of human error, enhance their security culture, and foster a workforce that is proactive and vigilant in safeguarding sensitive information.

Strategies for Building a Security-Aware Culture

In today's digital landscape, organizations face an ever-growing threat landscape that requires a proactive and vigilant approach to cybersecurity. Building a security-aware culture is crucial for mitigating risks and protecting sensitive information.

Leadership Commitment: Creating a security-aware culture starts at the top. Leaders within the organization must demonstrate a strong commitment to security and set the tone for the entire workforce. Executives should actively participate in security initiatives, communicate the importance of security to employees, and allocate resources to support security awareness programs. By leading by example, executives inspire employees to prioritize security and create a culture in which security is ingrained in every aspect of the organization's operations.

Communication and Training: Effective communication and training are essential for building a security-aware culture. Organizations should develop comprehensive security policies and procedures and communicate them clearly to all employees. Regular training sessions should be conducted to educate employees on security best practices, emerging threats, and their roles in safeguarding sensitive information. Training should be interactive, engaging, and tailored to different employee roles and levels of technical expertise. Communication channels such as newsletters, email updates, and posters can also be used to reinforce key security messages and keep employees informed.

Fostering Accountability: Building a security-aware culture requires a sense of individual and collective accountability. Employees should be encouraged to take ownership of their security responsibilities and understand the potential effects of their actions on the organization's overall security posture. Regular security assessments and evaluations can help identify areas for improvement and hold individuals and teams accountable for their security practices. Rewarding and recognizing employees who demonstrate exemplary security awareness reinforces the importance of security and encourages others to follow suit.

Continuous Improvement: Cybersecurity threats and best practices are constantly evolving, requiring organizations to prioritize continuous improvement. Regular assessments of the security-aware culture can help identify gaps and areas for enhancement. Feedback from employees should be encouraged and considered when refining security awareness programs. Monitoring and analyzing security metrics and incident trends can provide insights into the effectiveness of security measures and guide adjustments to the security-aware culture strategy. Embracing a mindset of continuous improvement ensures that the organization stays resilient in the face of evolving threats.

Embedding Security in Business Processes: To truly integrate security into the organizational culture, it is essential to embed security considerations into core business processes. Security should be considered from the early stages of project planning and design rather than being an afterthought. Incorporating security requirements into development methodologies, procurement processes, and third-party vendor assessments ensures that security is not compromised. By making security an integral part of daily operations, organizations can foster a security-aware culture that permeates throughout the organization.

Collaboration and Communication Channels

Collaboration and effective communication channels play a crucial role in building a security-aware culture. Encouraging cross-functional collaboration among security teams, IT departments, and other business units enhances knowledge sharing and promotes a holistic approach to security. Creating forums for employees to share security-related concerns, insights, and success stories allows for continuous learning and improvement. Implementing secure communication channels and incident-reporting mechanisms ensures that employees have a means to report potential security incidents promptly. Collaboration among different stakeholders within an organization is crucial for addressing security challenges holistically. By bringing together individuals from various departments, including IT, security, operations, and management, organizations can leverage diverse expertise to develop comprehensive security strategies. Collaborative efforts facilitate the identification of vulnerabilities, the sharing of threat intelligence, and the development of proactive security measures. Furthermore, collaboration promotes a collective responsibility for security, fostering a culture in which employees are actively engaged in safeguarding the organization's digital assets.

Effective communication channels are essential for disseminating critical security information throughout the organization. Timely and accurate communication ensures that employees are aware of emerging threats, policy updates, and best practices. It enables the quick dissemination of security alerts, incident response protocols, and recovery procedures. Clear and concise communication reduces the likelihood of misunderstandings and enables swift action during security incidents. Moreover, communication channels serve as a platform for employees to seek guidance, report suspicious activities, and share security-related concerns, fostering a culture of open communication and collaboration.

Strategies for establishing effective collaboration and communication channels include the following:

- **Cross-functional teams:** Forming cross-functional teams that bring together representatives from different departments can promote collaboration and information sharing. These teams can work on security projects, conduct risk assessments, and develop security policies and procedures that are aligned with the organization's goals.

- **Training and awareness programs:** Implementing regular training and awareness programs on security practices ensures that employees understand their roles and responsibilities. These programs can include workshops, seminars, and e-learning modules that cover topics such as phishing awareness, password hygiene, and social engineering.

- **Secure communication tools:** Using secure communication tools such as encrypted email services, instant messaging platforms, and collaboration software helps protect sensitive information during digital interactions. These tools should be implemented with proper access controls and user-authentication mechanisms.

- **Incident-reporting mechanisms:** Establishing confidential and user-friendly incident-reporting mechanisms encourages employees to report security incidents or suspicious activities promptly. Anonymity and nonretaliation policies should be in place to ensure that employees feel safe and supported when reporting potential security incidents.

- **Security awareness campaigns:** Security awareness campaigns can help reinforce the importance of protecting digital assets and engage employees in proactive security practices. These campaigns can include posters, newsletters, and regular security reminders that highlight emerging threats, security tips, and success stories.

- **Regular communication channels:** Establishing regular communication channels, such as security newsletters, intranet portals, and dedicated security email groups, allows for the dissemination of security-related information to employees. These channels should be used to provide updates on security incidents, policy changes, and best practices.

- **Collaborative platforms:** Leveraging collaborative platforms such as project management tools and document-sharing platforms enables secure collaboration among teams. These platforms should include security features such as access controls and encryption to safeguard sensitive information.

Establishing effective collaboration and communication channels is essential for enhancing security in the digital age. By fostering collaboration among stakeholders and implementing secure communication channels, organizations can strengthen their defenses against cyberthreats. The strategies outlined provide a framework for organizations to establish a culture of collaboration, information sharing, and open communication. By prioritizing collaboration and effective communication, businesses can create a security-aware environment in which employees are equipped with the knowledge and resources to protect the organization's digital assets.

Building a security-aware culture is an ongoing journey that requires commitment, communication, training, accountability, continuous improvement, and integration of security into business processes. By cultivating a culture in which security is valued and ingrained in every employee's mindset, organizations can significantly strengthen their defense against cyberthreats. A security-aware culture ensures that employees are equipped with the knowledge and skills to identify and respond to potential security risks, making them active participants in safeguarding the organization's valuable assets. With the right strategies and a collective commitment to securing digital resources, organizations can establish a robust security-aware culture that mitigates risks and promotes a secure and resilient environment.

Chapter 12:
Employee Education and Awareness

The role of employees in ensuring cybersecurity and data protection has taken center stage. Employee education and awareness have emerged as crucial pillars for guarding organizations against a myriad of cyber threats and breaches. This chapter delves into the paramount importance of employee education and awareness, elucidating the reasons for its necessity, the multitude of benefits it bestows, and the potential it holds for the future of organizational security.

The cyber threat landscape is constantly evolving, with cybercriminals becoming increasingly sophisticated in their tactics. As a result, organizations find themselves grappling with an array of threats, including phishing attacks, social engineering, malware infections, and insider threats. Although technology plays a significant role in fortifying an organization's defense, it is the human element that can be both the strongest and weakest link. Recognizing this, the need for a well-informed and vigilant workforce becomes evident. The importance of employee education and awareness lies in the fact that it equips employees with the knowledge and tools to recognize and mitigate these threats effectively.

The benefits of comprehensive employee education and awareness programs ripple through various dimensions of an organization. First, they serve as a preventive measure, empowering employees to identify potential security risks and take proactive steps to prevent breaches. By being able to discern phishing emails, suspicious links, and social engineering attempts, employees serve as an early line of defense, significantly reducing the likelihood of successful attacks. Additionally, a well-educated workforce fosters a security-conscious culture in which security practices become second nature. This leads to improved compliance with security protocols and regulations.

A tangible benefit of employee education and awareness is the reduction in security incidents and breaches. The 2021 "Cost of a Data Breach Report" by IBM revealed that organizations with comprehensive security awareness training programs experienced 76 percent fewer breaches than those without such programs. This substantial decrease in breach incidents translates into saved costs, preserved reputations, and maintained customer trust. The importance of employee education and awareness in bolstering an organization's cybersecurity defenses cannot be overstated. To fortify the human element of security, organizations must implement comprehensive strategies to educate and raise awareness among their employees.

This chapter delves into a detailed exploration of the steps an organization can undertake to effectively educate and raise awareness, ensuring that employees become active contributors to the organization's cybersecurity posture.

Assessment and Understanding of Needs

Before embarking on an employee education and awareness program, organizations must thoroughly assess their existing cybersecurity posture. According to the 2020 *Verizon Data Breach Investigations Report*, 22 percent of data breaches were caused by human error. By identifying specific vulnerabilities and threat vectors, organizations can tailor their education efforts accordingly. This initial step is foundational to crafting a strategy that addresses the most pertinent risks to the organization.

Developing Tailored Programs

A one-size-fits-all approach is not effective when it comes to employee education. Metrics from a study by the Security Awareness Company found that 75 percent of organizations offer some form of cybersecurity training, yet only 38 percent of employees felt that training was helpful. This highlights the need for customized programs based on employees' roles and understanding levels. For instance, a marketing employee might need different training from what an IT administrator needs. Tailored programs ensure that education is relevant and engaging.

Leadership Buy-In and Support

The importance of organizational leadership's buy-in cannot be overstated. A report by IBM showed that organizations with strong cybersecurity cultures are 52 percent less likely to experience a data breach. Leadership involvement demonstrates the seriousness of cybersecurity to the entire workforce. By participating in training sessions and endorsing security practices, leaders set a clear example for employees to follow.

Creating Engaging Content

Engaging content is crucial for effective education. Interactive workshops, simulation exercises, and real-world case studies make learning immersive and enjoyable. Metrics from a study by the SANS Institute found that organizations that used gamification in their training programs saw a 60 percent improvement in employee engagement. These methods also lead to higher retention rates of employees, which ultimately translate into better security practices.

Fostering a Security-Conscious Culture

As discussed in the previous chapter, a security-conscious culture is a cornerstone of successful employee education and awareness programs. The 2021 "State of Security Awareness Report" showed that organizations with a strong security culture experience 90 percent fewer security-related incidents. Employees should understand that cybersecurity is everyone's responsibility. Real-world examples of companies such as Google that have security as part of their core values showcase how a security-conscious culture permeates every aspect of the organization.

Regular Training and Refreshers

The evolving threat landscape requires ongoing education. Metrics from a report by CyberSafe revealed that 64 percent of employees admitted to using the same password for multiple accounts. Regular training sessions and refresher courses keep employees informed about the latest threats and mitigation strategies. This consistent effort ensures that employees remain vigilant over time.

Simulated Phishing Exercises

Metrics from the 2020 State of the Phish Report revealed that 88 percent of organizations experienced phishing attacks. Simulated phishing exercises allow organizations to gauge their employees' susceptibility to such attacks. By tracking metrics related to click rates on simulated phishing emails, organizations can identify areas where further education is needed and measure improvements over time. A study by CSO Online found that 53 percent of employees who received simulated phishing emails engaged with them.

Rewarding Good Behavior

Positive reinforcement can significantly influence employee behavior. Recognizing and rewarding employees who exhibit good cybersecurity practices can create a sense of competition and pride in adhering to security protocols. This can range from simple recognition in team meetings to tangible rewards. Implementing positive reinforcement through rewards for good behavior can significantly influence employee engagement.

Measuring Effectiveness

Measuring the effectiveness of an education and awareness program in the realm of cybersecurity extends beyond mere quantitative metrics; it involves a nuanced evaluation of various key performance indicators. Reduced incident rates, indicative of the program's impact on mitigating security breaches, stand as a primary benchmark of success. Similarly, the improved identification of phishing emails during simulated exercises underscores the enhanced resilience of employees against social engineering tactics, highlighting the program's efficacy in fostering a vigilant workforce. Additionally, the increased adoption of secure practices signifies the integration of cybersecurity awareness into daily routines, a pivotal outcome in fortifying an organization's overall digital posture. Regularly scrutinizing these metrics not only provides valuable insights into the program's tangible impact but also facilitates the identification of specific areas for improvement. Furthermore, metrics pertaining to the utilization of clear reporting channels for suspicious activities offer a qualitative dimension, enabling organizations to gauge the effectiveness of their communication strategies in fostering a transparent and responsive cybersecurity culture. By embracing a holistic approach to measuring effectiveness, organizations can refine their education and awareness initiatives to align seamlessly with the ever-evolving cybersecurity landscape.

Feedback and Continuous Improvement

Regularly soliciting feedback from employees about the effectiveness of the training programs is essential. Their insights can provide valuable information about what is working and what needs improvement. This feedback loop supports continuous improvement in the education and awareness initiatives.

Integration with Onboarding and Training

Metrics from the Security Awareness Company showed that 70 percent of employees say they lack cybersecurity knowledge. Integrating cybersecurity education into the onboarding process establishes a strong foundation for new employees. Additionally, incorporating cybersecurity training into broader training initiatives ensures consistent messaging about security throughout an employee's journey.

The future of employee education and awareness holds even greater promise. As the threat landscape continues to evolve, so must the education and training provided to employees. With the rise of remote work and the internet of things (IoT), new attack vectors are emerging. Employees need to be educated about the security implications of remote-work practices and how IoT devices can introduce vulnerabilities into an organization's network. In the coming years, AI and ML will likely be integrated into employee education. These technologies can be used to personalize training programs, adapting content to the individual's learning pace and preferences. Moreover, gamification and interactive learning methods are likely to become more prevalent, enhancing engagement and retention of security practices.

In conclusion, employee education and awareness are the linchpin of modern organizational security. The need for a workforce well versed in cybersecurity practices has never been greater, given the complex and evolving nature of cyberthreats. The benefits span from preventive measures to tangible reductions in security incidents and breaches. Real-world examples underscore the difference that education can make, and metrics highlight the financial advantages it brings. The future of employee education and awareness holds the promise of innovation, personalization, and the continued evolution of a security-conscious culture. Organizations that prioritize this aspect will be better equipped to navigate the ever-changing cybersecurity landscape, safeguarding their data, reputation, and stakeholder trust.

Chapter 13:
Regulatory Compliance and Governance

In an increasingly digitized world, organizations face numerous challenges in ensuring the security and privacy of sensitive data. Regulatory compliance and governance play a critical role in helping businesses navigate the complex landscape of data protection and meet legal obligations. This chapter explores the importance of regulatory compliance and governance in safeguarding data, outlines key regulations and frameworks, and provides insights into best practices for achieving compliance and effective governance. Regulatory compliance is the adherence to laws, regulations, and industry standards that govern data protection, privacy, and security. It is essential for organizations to comply with these regulations to maintain the trust of customers, protect sensitive information, and avoid legal and financial penalties.

Compliance provides a framework for organizations to establish robust data protection measures, implement risk management practices, and demonstrate a commitment to maintaining data integrity and confidentiality. Additionally, effective governance ensures that policies, procedures, and controls are in place to enforce compliance and mitigate risks effectively. In today's complex and interconnected business landscape, regulatory compliance and governance have become critical components of organizational success. The increasing volume and sensitivity of data, along with the growing number of regulations and industry standards, necessitate a proactive and diligent approach to ensure compliance.

Conformance with applicable laws, regulations, and standards is not only a legal requirement but also vital for maintaining the trust of stakeholders, protecting sensitive information, and avoiding significant reputational and financial risks. One of the primary reasons regulatory compliance and governance are crucial is the protection of sensitive data. Many organizations handle vast amounts of data, including personal information, financial records, and trade secrets. Adhering to regulations such as the GDPR, CCPA, and PCI DSS ensures that organizations have robust security measures in place to safeguard this data. By complying with these regulations, organizations demonstrate their commitment to protecting the privacy and confidentiality of individuals' information, which enhances customer trust and loyalty.

Furthermore, regulatory compliance and governance help organizations mitigate legal and financial risks. Noncompliance with regulations can result in severe consequences, including fines, penalties, and legal actions. These repercussions can significantly affect an organization's finances, reputation, and overall business operations. By implementing effective compliance programs and governance structures, organizations can identify and address potential risks, reducing the likelihood of noncompliance and associated penalties.

Compliance with regulations also enhances an organization's reputation and credibility. In an era when data breaches and privacy incidents regularly make headlines, consumers and stakeholders have become more conscious of how organizations handle their data. Being compliant with relevant regulations signifies that an organization takes data protection seriously, thereby establishing a positive reputation for trustworthiness. This reputation can attract more customers, strengthen existing relationships, and provide a competitive advantage in the market. Moreover, regulatory compliance and governance contribute to the overall efficiency and effectiveness of an organization. Compliance requirements often necessitate the implementation of robust policies, procedures, and controls.

These measures help streamline business operations, ensure consistency, and minimize errors. By adhering to industry standards and best practices, organizations can optimize their processes, improve data quality, and enhance operational resilience. Another significant benefit of regulatory compliance and governance is the ability to adapt to a rapidly changing business landscape. The regulatory environment is dynamic, with new regulations and standards being introduced regularly. Compliance programs help organizations stay up to date with the latest requirements and ensure that their practices align with changing regulations. This agility allows organizations to proactively address emerging risks, maintain compliance, and avoid disruptions to their operations.

Key Regulations and Frameworks

The primary regulations that apply to United States and international businesses and organizations providing information security and data privacy protection are the following:

- **General Data Protection Regulation (GDPR):** The GDPR, implemented in the European Union (EU), sets strict rules for the processing, storage, and transfer of the personal data of EU citizens. It grants individuals covered by GDPR greater control over their personal information and imposes hefty fines on public and private businesses and organizations for noncompliance.

- **California Consumer Privacy Act (CCPA):** The CCPA provides California residents with rights regarding their personal information and requires businesses to be transparent about their data practices. It applies to organizations that collect and process personal data of California residents.

- **Payment Card Industry Data Security Standard (PCI DSS):** PCI DSS is a set of security standards developed by major credit card companies to protect cardholder data. Compliance with PCI DSS is mandatory for organizations that handle payment card information.

- **Health Insurance Portability and Accountability Act (HIPAA):** HIPAA establishes privacy and security standards for protected health information in the health-care industry. Compliance is required for health-care providers, insurers, and business associates.

- **ISO/IEC 27001:** This international standard provides a framework for establishing an information security management system. It outlines a risk-based approach to identify, assess, and manage information security risks.

Best Practices for Achieving Compliance and Effective Governance

Ensuring compliance and effective governance involves using a strong system with constant monitoring, clear policies, and regular audits in the dynamic realm of cybersecurity.

- **Conduct regular risk assessments:** Organizations should regularly assess their data security risks and vulnerabilities to identify gaps in compliance. This includes conducting internal audits, vulnerability assessments, and penetration testing to proactively address security weaknesses. Penetration testing is a cybersecurity practice in computer science. It involves simulating a real-world cyberattack on a computer system, network, or application to identify vulnerabilities and weaknesses that malicious hackers could exploit.

- **Establish comprehensive policies and procedures:** Clear and comprehensive data protection policies and procedures should be developed and communicated across the organization. This includes defining roles and responsibilities, outlining data-handling practices, and implementing incident response plans.

- **Implement access controls and data encryption:** Access controls, including user authentication, role-based access, and privileged access management, should be implemented to restrict unauthorized access to sensitive data. Encryption techniques should also be used to protect data both in transit and at rest.

- **Train employees:** Regular training programs should be conducted to educate employees about regulatory requirements, data protection best practices, and the potential risks associated with noncompliance. Employees should be made aware of their roles in ensuring data privacy and security.

- **Create an incident response and breach notification plan:** Organizations should have a well-defined incident response plan in place to handle security incidents effectively. This includes clear procedures for identifying, containing, investigating, and reporting breaches to the relevant authorities and affected individuals, as required by law.

- **Audit regularly for compliance:** Regular compliance audits should be conducted to assess the effectiveness of security controls, policies, and procedures. These audits help identify areas of noncompliance and allow organizations to implement necessary remediation measures.

The Importance of Compliance and Effective Governance

Compliance with regulations and effective governance practices are vital for organizations to operate ethically, maintain trust, and mitigate risks. Best practices in achieving compliance and governance provide a framework for organizations to establish robust systems and processes that align with legal requirements, industry standards, and stakeholder expectations.

Here are key reasons why best practices for achieving compliance and effective governance are crucial:

- **Mitigating legal and reputational risks:** Compliance with laws and regulations is not just a legal requirement; it is also crucial for mitigating legal and reputational risks. Noncompliance can result in severe consequences such as fines, penalties, legal actions, and damage to an organization's reputation. By implementing best practices, organizations can ensure that they meet legal obligations, reduce the likelihood of noncompliance, and protect their reputation in the market. The following is a list of ten organizations and the amount each paid for cybersecurity noncompliance.

1. Google (2019): $56 million fine by the French Data Protection Authority for GDPR violations.

2. DoorDash (2019): $2.5 million settlement for a data breach compromising user data.

3. Capital One (2019): $80 million fine for a data breach affecting more than 100 million customers.

4. British Airways (2019): $26 million fine by the UK Information Commissioner's Office (ICO) for a data breach.

5. Facebook/Cambridge Analytica (2018): $5 billion settlement with the U.S. Federal Trade Commission for privacy violations.

6. Marriott (2018): $23.5 million fine by the UK ICO for a data breach.

7. Uber (2018): $491,000 fine by the UK ICO for poor data protection practices.

8. Equifax (2017): $700 million settlement for a data breach affecting 147 million people.

9. Yahoo (2017): $35 million settlement for failing to disclose a data breach.

10. Uber (2016): $148 million settlement for a data breach cover-up.

- **Ensuring data security and privacy:** Compliance with data protection regulations is of the utmost importance in today's digital age. Best practices help organizations establish robust data security and privacy measures to protect sensitive information from unauthorized access, breaches, and misuse. This includes implementing encryption, access controls, regular security audits, and incident response plans. By adhering to best practices, organizations can safeguard customer data, maintain trust, and avoid costly data breaches.

- **Enhancing stakeholder trust:** Compliance and effective governance practices contribute to building and maintaining trust with stakeholders such as customers, investors, employees, and business partners. When organizations demonstrate a commitment to ethical practices, transparency, and accountability, stakeholders feel more confident in their relationships with the organization. This trust can lead to increased customer loyalty, improved investor confidence, and stronger partnerships.

- **Streamlining processes and operations:** Best practices for compliance and governance often involve establishing standardized processes and controls. These practices help organizations streamline their operations, reduce redundancies, and improve efficiency. By implementing effective governance frameworks, organizations can ensure consistency in decision-making, optimize resource allocation, and minimize operational risks.

- **Facilitating business growth and expansion:** Compliance and effective governance are crucial for organizations looking to expand their operations or enter new markets. Many jurisdictions have specific regulations and requirements that organizations must meet to operate legally. By adopting best practices, organizations can ensure that they are well prepared to navigate regulatory landscapes and expand their business with confidence.

- **Fostering a culture of ethics and integrity:** Effective governance practices contribute to fostering a culture of ethics and integrity within an organization. By setting clear guidelines, promoting ethical behavior, and providing training and awareness programs, organizations can ensure that employees understand their responsibilities and act with integrity. Compliance programs often include training and awareness initiatives that educate employees about their responsibilities, ethical conduct, and the importance of data protection. This culture of ethics and integrity helps prevent misconduct, fraud, and unethical practices, ultimately protecting the organization's reputation and long-term success.

- **Adapting to changing regulatory landscapes:** The regulatory environment is dynamic, with regulations and requirements frequently evolving. Best practices for achieving compliance and effective governance enable organizations to stay updated with changing regulations and adapt their practices accordingly. This adaptability allows organizations to proactively address emerging risks, comply with new regulations, and avoid disruptions to their operations.

In conclusion, regulatory compliance and governance are essential for organizations operating in today's complex business environment. They provide a framework for organizations to protect sensitive data, mitigate legal and financial risks, enhance their reputation, improve operational efficiency, and foster a culture of ethics and integrity. By prioritizing regulatory compliance and governance, organizations can ensure long-term sustainability, trust, and success in an increasingly regulated world.

Chapter 14:
Continuous Improvement and Assessment

In the realm of cybersecurity, the continuous evaluation of customer feedback, meticulous performance assessments, and the proactive identification and resolution of quality gaps stand as indispensable pillars in the pursuit of digital fortification. Customer feedback serves as a real-time litmus test, providing invaluable insights into user experiences and potential vulnerabilities. By staying attuned to the evolving needs and concerns of end-users, cybersecurity measures can be refined to align seamlessly with the dynamic threat landscape. Simultaneously, systematic performance assessments offer a comprehensive view of the efficacy of existing security protocols, highlighting areas that demand enhancement or refinement. Identifying and promptly addressing gaps in quality not only bolsters the robustness of defense mechanisms but also fosters a culture of continuous improvement, ensuring that cybersecurity measures evolve in tandem with the ever-evolving tactics employed by malicious actors. In this interconnected digital ecosystem, where the stakes are high and the threat landscape is ever-shifting, the regular scrutiny of customer feedback and performance metrics becomes not just a best practice, but a strategic imperative for organizations committed to safeguarding their digital assets.

Continuous improvements involve seeking opportunities for growth, making incremental changes, and evaluating the effects of those changes to drive improvement. It goes beyond simple problem-solving; it focuses on ongoing efforts to achieve excellence and maximize organizational potential by enhancing processes, products, and services. Assessment involves evaluating performance and outcomes to drive improvement. This chapter explores the concepts of continuous improvement and assessment, their importance, and the benefits they bring to organizations. Continuous improvement and assessment have become crucial for corporations in today's fast-paced and competitive business environment.

These practices enable corporations to stay relevant, competitive, and successful. The importance of continuous improvement and assessment lies in their ability to enhance adaptability, agility, efficiency, and productivity within corporations. By continuously evaluating performance and gathering feedback, corporations can identify areas for improvement and make necessary adjustments swiftly. The resulting adaptability and agility allow corporations to meet customer demands effectively and maintain a competitive edge.

Moreover, continuous improvement initiatives help corporations identify and eliminate inefficiencies, streamline processes, and optimize resource use. By regularly assessing performance, corporations can identify bottlenecks, redundancies, and areas of waste. By addressing these issues, corporations can enhance efficiency, reduce costs, and improve overall productivity. Continuous improvement and assessment also enable corporations to focus on delivering high-quality products and services.

This commitment to quality leads to higher customer satisfaction, increased customer loyalty, and positive brand reputation. These practices also foster a culture of innovation within corporations. By encouraging employees to think creatively, experiment with new ideas, and challenge the status quo, corporations can drive innovation and fuel growth. Regular assessment provides valuable insights into the success of new initiatives, allowing corporations to refine and scale ideas that prove to be successful. Identifying and addressing skill gaps in cybersecurity personnel is essential for building a resilient and effective defense against cyber threats, ensuring ongoing professional development, and managing and securing digital assets.

Continuous improvement and assessment empower employees by involving them in the process of identifying improvement opportunities. This engagement fosters a sense of ownership, boosts morale, and encourages collaboration. Employees who are actively involved in continuous improvement initiatives are more motivated, productive, and invested in the corporation's success. These practices assist corporations in identifying and mitigating risks before they escalate. Regular evaluation of processes and systems allows corporations to detect vulnerabilities, address compliance issues, and implement preventive measures. By proactively managing risks, corporations can safeguard their reputation, protect assets, and ensure regulatory compliance.

Continuous improvement and assessment provide corporations with a competitive advantage in the market. By constantly striving for improvement, corporations can differentiate themselves from competitors, deliver superior products and services, and enhance customer experiences. This competitive advantage leads to increased market share, customer loyalty, and long-term sustainability. Continuous improvement and assessment provide corporations with data-driven insights to inform decision-making and align strategies with organizational goals. By collecting and analyzing relevant data, corporations can identify trends, patterns, and areas for improvement. This information enables informed decision-making, helps set realistic targets, and ensures that strategies are aligned with the corporation's vision and objectives.

Continuous improvement plays a crucial role in organizational success for several reasons:

- **Enhanced efficiency and effectiveness:** Continuous improvement drives efficiency by eliminating waste, reducing errors, and optimizing processes. It helps organizations identify bottlenecks, streamline workflows, and improve productivity. By continuously seeking ways to enhance effectiveness, organizations can meet customer needs more efficiently, deliver higher-quality products and services, and gain a competitive edge.

- **Innovation and adaptability:** Continuous improvement encourages innovation by fostering a culture of creativity and experimentation. It provides a platform for employees to suggest and implement new ideas, technologies, and processes. This enables organizations to adapt to changing market conditions, customer preferences, and technological advancements, staying ahead of the competition.

- **Customer satisfaction and loyalty:** Continuous improvement focuses on meeting and exceeding customer expectations. By constantly seeking feedback, evaluating customer needs, and making improvements, organizations can enhance customer satisfaction and loyalty. Satisfied customers become advocates for the organization, attracting new business and driving growth.

- **Employee engagement and empowerment:** Continuous improvement empowers employees by involving them in the process of identifying problems, suggesting solutions, and implementing changes. This engagement fosters a sense of ownership, boosts morale, and creates a collaborative work environment. Engaged employees are more motivated, productive, and committed to the organization's success.

Effective Assessment Practices

Assessment is an integral part of the continuous improvement process. It involves gathering data, analyzing performance, and evaluating outcomes to inform decision-making and drive improvement efforts. Effective assessment practices provide organizations with valuable insights into their strengths, weaknesses, and areas for improvement.

The following practices are key to effective assessment programs:

- **Establishing clear goals and key performance indicators (KPIs):** Organizations should define clear goals and KPIs that align with their strategic objectives. Some examples include unidentified devices on the network, intrusion attempts, mean time to detect, and mean time to resolve. These metrics help assess performance and provide a benchmark for improvement efforts. Regularly reviewing and updating KPIs ensures they remain relevant and reflective of organizational priorities.

- **Data collection and analysis:** Organizations must collect accurate and relevant data to assess performance. This data can be gathered through various methods, including surveys, interviews, observations, and performance metrics. Analyzing the data allows organizations to identify trends, patterns, and areas of improvement.

- **Feedback mechanisms:** Effective assessment involves seeking feedback from various stakeholders, including customers, employees, and partners. Feedback can be collected through surveys, focus groups, suggestion boxes, and performance evaluations. Incorporating diverse perspectives provides a comprehensive understanding of organizational strengths and areas for improvement.

- **Performance reviews and benchmarking:** Conducting periodic performance reviews allows organizations to assess progress, identify gaps, and set targets for improvement. Benchmarking against industry standards and best practices provides valuable insights into where the organization stands relative to its competitors and helps identify areas for improvement.

Benefits of Continuous Improvement and Assessment

Continuous improvement and assessment offer several benefits to organizations:

- **Competitive advantage:** By consistently improving processes, products, and services, organizations can differentiate themselves from competitors. They can deliver higher quality, increase efficiency, and meet changing customer demands more effectively, giving them a competitive edge in the market.

- **Cost savings:** Continuous improvement efforts help identify and eliminate inefficiencies, reducing operational costs. Streamlined processes, reduced waste, and improved productivity result in significant cost savings over time.

- **Organizational learning:** Continuous improvement encourages a culture of learning and development within the organization. Through assessment, organizations can identify knowledge gaps, invest in training and development programs, and foster a learning environment that promotes individual and organizational growth.

- **Risk mitigation:** Continuous improvement and assessment help identify and address potential risks to cybersecurity before they escalate. By regularly assessing processes and systems, organizations can detect vulnerabilities, implement preventive measures, and ensure compliance with regulations and standards.

Implementing continuous improvement and assessment within an organization can be a challenging endeavor. There are various obstacles that corporations may face, ranging from resistance to change to resource limitations. However, by proactively addressing these challenges, organizations can unlock the benefits of continuous improvement and assessment to drive growth, efficiency, and innovation.

One of the primary challenges is resistance to change. Many employees may be comfortable with existing processes and reluctant to embrace change. This can result in pushback, lack of engagement, and a reluctance to participate in improvement initiatives. To overcome this challenge, organizations need to foster a culture of openness and collaboration. This can be achieved through effective change management strategies, including clear communication, stakeholder involvement, and providing training and support to employees. By involving employees in the process and demonstrating the value of continuous improvement, organizations can overcome resistance and create a culture that embraces change and innovation.

Another challenge is the lack of a structured approach to continuous improvement and assessment. Without a well-defined framework, organizations may struggle to identify areas for improvement, establish clear goals, and measure progress. To address this challenge, corporations should adopt established improvement methodologies such as Six Sigma, Lean, or Agile. These frameworks provide a structured and systematic approach to continuous improvement, guiding organizations through the steps of identifying opportunities, analyzing data, implementing changes, and monitoring outcomes. By adopting a proven methodology, organizations can ensure a disciplined approach to improvement and effectively measure the effects of their efforts.

Resource limitations can also pose a significant challenge to implementing continuous improvement and assessment. Organizations may face constraints in terms of budget, personnel, or technology. Lack of resources can hinder the ability to invest in improvement initiatives, allocate dedicated personnel, or acquire necessary tools and technologies. To overcome this challenge, corporations need to prioritize and allocate resources strategically. This can involve securing executive sponsorship and support for improvement initiatives, leveraging cross-functional teams to share resources and expertise, and making use of cost-effective technology solutions. By making resource allocation a priority and optimizing the available resources, organizations can effectively implement continuous improvement and assessment initiatives.

Another obstacle is the lack of data and metrics for assessment. Without accurate and reliable data, organizations may struggle to measure progress, identify trends, and make data-driven decisions. It is essential for organizations to establish a robust data-collection and analysis process. This involves identifying relevant KPIs that align with organizational goals, implementing systems and processes to capture data, and regularly reviewing and analyzing the data to derive insights. Organizations can leverage technology solutions such as business intelligence tools or data analytics platforms to facilitate data collection, analysis, and reporting. By establishing a data-driven approach to assessment, organizations can gain valuable insights, track improvement efforts, and make informed decisions.

Resistance from organizational silos can also hinder the implementation of continuous improvement and assessment. In large organizations, different departments or business units may operate independently and be resistant to sharing information or collaborating on improvement initiatives. This siloed mentality can limit the organization's ability to identify cross-functional improvement opportunities and hinder the sharing of best practices. To overcome this challenge, organizations need to foster a culture of collaboration and knowledge sharing. This can involve establishing cross-functional teams, facilitating communication channels, and implementing systems for sharing insights, lessons learned, and success stories. By breaking down silos and promoting collaboration, organizations can tap into the collective knowledge and experience of their employees to drive continuous improvement.

Implementing continuous improvement and assessment within an organization is not without its challenges. However, by proactively addressing these challenges, organizations can unlock the benefits of continuous improvement and assessment, such as increased efficiency, innovation, and growth. By overcoming resistance to change, adopting structured approaches, allocating resources strategically, leveraging data and metrics, and fostering collaboration, corporations can establish a culture of continuous improvement and drive sustainable success. Embracing continuous improvement and assessment as an ongoing process will enable organizations to adapt to changing market conditions, enhance operational effectiveness, and remain competitive in today's dynamic business landscape.

This approach is vital for organizations aiming to achieve excellence, adapt to change, and drive success. By fostering a culture of continuous improvement, organizations can enhance efficiency, innovation, customer satisfaction, and employee engagement. Effective assessment practices provide valuable insights into organizational performance, enabling data-driven decision-making and targeted improvement efforts. Embracing continuous improvement and assessment as ongoing processes allows organizations to stay competitive, mitigate risks, and achieve long-term growth and success. They provide a framework for corporations to adapt, improve efficiency, enhance quality, foster innovation, engage employees, manage risks, gain a competitive advantage, and make informed decisions. By embracing continuous improvement and implementing effective assessment practices, corporations can drive growth and achieve operational excellence.

Conclusion

In the pages of this comprehensive guide, we have embarked on a journey through the intricate world of cybersecurity for enterprises. This book has served as a road map, leading you through each crucial aspect of safeguarding the digital fortresses that modern businesses have become. As we conclude our exploration, let's reflect on the valuable insights we hope you have gained from each chapter. Our voyage commenced with a deep dive into the world of cybersecurity. We've come to understand that it's not merely a technological challenge but a strategic necessity. In the digital age, when data is a precious asset and cyberthreats are omnipresent, the importance of a robust cybersecurity posture cannot be overstated. Next, we guided you through the process of identifying and assessing risks, emphasizing the proactive nature of threat modeling. We've pointed out that anticipating potential threats and vulnerabilities allows organizations to develop tailored mitigation strategies, a cornerstone of effective cybersecurity.

Then we discussed the development of a strategic cybersecurity plan. Crafting a strategy aligned with organizational objectives is essential, and we've seen that effective leadership support, a well-defined road map, and constant evaluation are integral to achieving this alignment. We then focused on the significance of security policies and procedures. These documents not only lay out the rules but also provide a structured framework for responding to security incidents. We explained that clear guidelines are pivotal to a robust cybersecurity posture. Later we led you into the technical domain of cybersecurity. We elucidated the importance of network and infrastructure security, highlighting the necessity of proactive measures to prevent unauthorized access and data breaches. Then we explored the challenges posed by the cloud, a pivotal component of modern IT infrastructure. Chapter 9 illuminated the importance of encryption, access control, and compliance considerations in ensuring the security of cloud-based resources. Following that, we examined the mobile landscape, recognizing the omnipresence of smartphones and tablets. We went on to underscore the importance of identity and access management. Realizing that it covers the critical components of user authentication, authorization, and privilege management, we emphasized the importance of ensuring that access to vital resources is controlled and monitored. In an effort to deepen your understanding of the importance of an incident response plan, we illuminated the necessity of a well-defined strategy to minimize damage and ensure business continuity in the event of a security breach. Additionally, we addressed the human factor in cybersecurity. We explained that fostering a security-conscious organizational culture through effective training programs is pivotal to preventing threats from within.

Next, we delved into the complexities of managing risks associated with external partners. We highlighted the importance of thorough assessments, due diligence, and contractual considerations in mitigating these risks. Furthermore, we navigated through the intricate realm of regulatory compliance and governance. We emphasized adherence to industry-specific regulations and frameworks as a fundamental element of a robust security posture. Equally important, we looked at the import of daily operations of a cybersecurity program. We explored the significance of continuous monitoring, coordinated incident responses, and the integration of security information and event management systems. Our journey ended with an understanding of the need for perpetual enhancement in cybersecurity. We identified metrics, KPIs, and regular assessments as tools for adaptation and strengthening of security strategies over time.

As you conclude your voyage through the pages of this comprehensive guide, we hope you emerge equipped with a holistic understanding of cybersecurity for enterprises. Whether you are a seasoned cybersecurity practitioner or a novice, our intention was to provide invaluable insights and practical wisdom to secure your organization's digital assets in an ever-evolving digital landscape. In the face of evolving threats, your strategies must evolve too, and we hope this book has empowered you to embrace this ongoing challenge with confidence and competence.

www.ingramcontent.com/pod-product-compliance
Lightning Source LLC
LaVergne TN
LVHW021823060526
838201LV00058B/3493